EARTH worms
IN NEW ZEALAND

EARTH worms
IN NEW ZEALAND
Life Beneath the Surface

Amy Brown

REED

Published by Reed Books, a division of Reed Publishing (NZ) Ltd, 39 Rawene Road, Birkenhead, Auckland. Associated companies, branches and representatives throughout the world.

This book is copyright. Except for the purpose of fair reviewing, no part of this publication may be reproduced or transmitted in any form or by any means, electronic or mechanical, including photocopying, recording, or any information storage and retrieval system, without permission in writing from the publisher. Infringers of copyright render themselves liable to prosecution.

ISBN 0 7900 0446 1

© Amy Brown 1995
Designed by Clair Stutton
Cover illustration by Zoë Nash
Illustrations by Mark Roman

First published 1995

Printed in New Zealand

Dedicated with affection to all the worms I have handled, as well as the ones I have known.

Thanks are due to all the soil science and earthworm researcher types, especially Dr Jo Springett of AgResearch.

CONTENTS

PART I

The subterranean world of earthworms	11
Earthworms in New Zealand	14
What do earthworms need?	20
Passing the time	24
Soil — the living environment	30
Earthworms — the great transformers	35

PART II

New Zealand as an earthworm-friendly environment	47
Speeding up the transformation	49
Earthworms in the garden	57
Earthworms in pasture	66
Putting it into practice	82
Earthworms in orchards and foodcrops	85
Earthworm farming	94
New Zealand worm farmers	103
Bibliography	108

PART I

The Subterranean World of Earthworms

In the earth beneath our feet, the pint-sized but Herculean little earthworm is a major player in the subterranean world which influences our environment and has a significant effect on our health and economy.

Since earthworms evolved from their original marine environment to live in the earth they have survived without major changes, but with modified features that are adapted to exotic foods in a range of soils in different parts of the world. This adaptability explains the distribution of over 3,000 species throughout the world.

Whatever species they are, wherever they are found, and whether they are composters or earthworkers, the earthworm's purpose in life is to devour organic material and soil and excrete it, after its passage through the body, as soil-friendly, mineral-enriched castings or humus, quite simply the best topsoil builder in the world.

Around 192 species of earthworms, mainly native, occur in New Zealand. According to K.E. Lee, writing in a DSIR bulletin in

> Earthworms belong to the family Annelida and class Chaetopoda. Annelida, from anellus, a ring, is descriptive of the muscular rings on the earthworm's body, which can number up to 400; Chaetopoda — meaning bristle feet — refers to the bristle-like accessories or setae, which help earthworms go about their peripatetic existence.

1959, 'it is most likely that New Zealand [native] earthworms came originally from the Indo-Malayan or Australian region and entered New Zealand across a land connection from the north'.

Despite the high number of species, only about eight introduced genera are of critical importance to our pastures, croplands and gardens. The native earthworms, with a few deep-burrowing subsoil exceptions, were too specialised to adjust and their populations quickly decreased once the forest was felled or fired and the land cultivated.

Over the years many people have shared an enthusiasm for earthworms, including Charles Darwin, whose interest in these small creatures extended over 70 years. He first read his paper 'On the Formation of Vegetable Mould' to the Geological Society of London in 1837.

One of Darwin's studies lasted for 29 years, beginning in 1842 when a quantity of chalk was laid over part of a field near his house. Darwin wanted to see how long it would take the chalk to become buried. In 1871 a trench dug across the field revealed a line of white nodules, the remains of the chalk, about 18 centimetres below the surface. This reinforced Darwin's theory that earthworms created topsoil. Ten years later Darwin estimated that the 65,000 or so earthworms which populated each hectare of pasture in Kent would bring between 22 and 45 tonnes of worm casts, or reconstituted soil, to the surface of the land each year.

Darwin's work caused interest in New Zealand too, and an early description of a New Zealand earthworm was recorded by L.K. Schmarda in 1861. A.T. Urquhart and W.W. Smith were stimulated by Darwin's work, as was Sir W.B. Benham, who published his first paper on New Zealand Megascolecidae in 1891 and continued publishing until 1949.

Early in the 1930s A.S. Ashmore began to systematically 'plant' *Aporrectodea caliginosa* on his paddocks in the Raetihi district, leading in 1945 to what I understand was the first New Zealand study showing that plant growth can be increased and soil structure improved by earthworms.

— *The subterranean world of earthworms* —

Since then many of our soil scientists have carried out notable and innovative research on pasture earthworms — the soil dwellers and builders — the results of which carry implications of huge importance to the New Zealand farming economy. It is difficult to understand why their recommendations have not been adopted by more farmers. Perhaps farmers have not believed the results, or it may be because the recipes for increased pasture growth and carrying capacity are not 'quick fix' methods. Perhaps the research is not readily available. Whatever the reason it is worthwhile encouraging farmers, cropgrowers and gardeners to utilise the earthworm as an important tool because one fact is paramount — earthworms have important effects on soil productivity and fertility.

While there are soil scientists eager to spend their time in productive earthworm research, they are continually frustrated by a lack of funding and the 'user pays' philosophy. If New Zealand farmers and cropgrowers would utilise the scientists' knowledge and apply their research they could earn a robust living, while New Zealand could lead the world in organic farming management.

My quest for information and my haphazard experiments continue to leave me with an enduring respect and admiration for these small denizens of the earth. A couple of years ago a 90-year-old man from the deep south sent me a postcard he had kept for many decades. It showed Darwin's millstone, left for years on pasture near his home at Beckenham, which he was gratified to find was being covered to the extent of one centimetre of topsoil every four years. On the back of the postcard Jack wrote, 'Worms are quieter and a damn sight more useful than most men.'

Earthworms in New Zealand

The smallest known native earthworm in New Zealand is the non-burrowing leaf-mould dweller *Diporochaeta punctata*, 14–18 mm in length and 1–1.5 mm in diameter. The largest is the subsoil dweller *Spenceriella gigantea*, 1,300–1,400 mm in length and around 11 mm in diameter, which makes burrows of up to 20 mm in diameter. (Their relative sizes are illustrated below.)

You may have come across other thriving leaf-mould species in native forest, manuka stands, or other regenerating bush areas, topsoil and tussockland dwellers, and species living in and around swamps and wetland areas. Some native species still thrive but most remain as reduced and remnant populations.

The imported lumbricids which have largely replaced the indigenous species have not penetrated to all areas

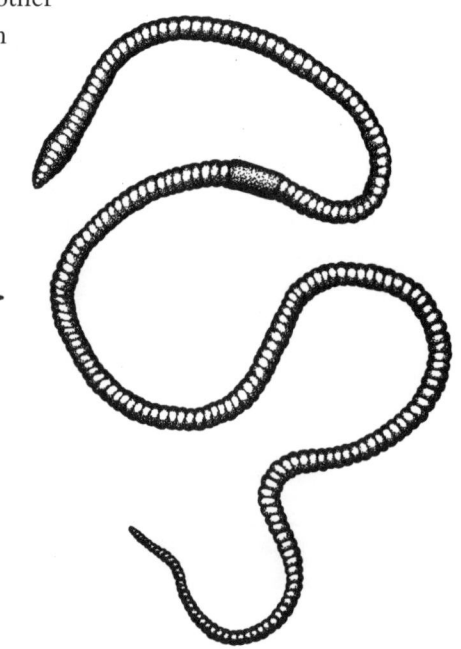

of the country, but as long ago as the late 1880s Smith and Urquhart were reporting on their distribution. While eight genera endure we will only concern ourselves with the most useful for agriculture and composting, *Aporrectodea, Lumbricus, Eisenia* and *Octolasium*.

VALUABLE IMPORTED EARTHWORMS

Earthworkers

Colour	Size (cm)	Depth (cm)	Habitat
Aporrectodea caliginosa			
grey, brown, pink	up to 10	usu. 15–30	pasture, gardens, orchards, cropland, leaves

Improves soil structure and fertility, breaks down root-mat, incorporates fertilisers into soil. Horizontal U-shaped burrow enables surface casting. Body straight but pointed.

Aporrectodea trapezoides			
purple, brown/grey; tail slightly flattened	up to 10	20–30	pasture

Reproduces slowly. Needs adequate rainfall. Good soil improver; surface feeder but will take material deep. Does not like heavy grazing. Casts in burrow.

Aporrectodea longa			
grey-brown, pale yellow; pink head, iridescent; tail slightly flattened	up to 18	25–50	pasture, farmland

Not normally found near surface. Very desirable because of deep mixing of subsoil minerals with topsoil. Casts in burrow.

Aporrectodea rosea (Rosytip)			
yellowish, pink head, pale tail	up to 10	20–30	gardens, pasture

Good soil mixer, but seldom feeds on surface. Has rosy flattish tip on tail end. Casts in burrow.

Aporrectodea chlorotica			
pale or dark green or greenish yellow	up to 8	12–18	gardens, pasture

Good soil mixer, agile and flicks around. Will coil if disturbed. Doesn't mind waterlogged soil. Casts in burrows. Smelly.

Colour	Size (cm)	Depth (cm)	Habitat
Octolasium cyaneum			
bluish-grey, yellow tip to tail	up to 16	15–20	pasture forest
Found in low-fertility soils and remnant native forests surrounded by pasture.			
Lumbricus terrestris			
Iridescent, pink/brown	up to 30	commonly 45 sometimes 170–180 occas. 360–400	garden paddock orchard leaves
Largest imported worm. Surface feeder, pulls leaves, chocolate into burrow. Great subsoil mixer. U-shaped burrow which enables casting on surface. Loved by fishers.			

Compost worms

Lumbricus rubellus (Red worm)

Red, maroon, yellowish; flattish tail	up to 12	12	pasture compost manure
Prolific breeder with up to 60 capsules per year. Surface feeder. Great cultivated worm and castings producer. Likes compost, manure, heavy organics and damp soil. Good fishing worm. Casts near to surface.			

Eisenia foetida (Tiger worm)

red and yellow bands	up to 10	6–12	compost manure sewage
Poor pasture worm. Best cultivated worm and rapid castings producer. Can breed up to 60 times a year. Rapid body growth. Casts near to surface. Reputedly unpopular with fishers because of yellow excreted substance but this overcome by purging in damp oatmeal or bran.			

Aporrectodea caliginosa (either *forma typica* or *trapezoides*) is one of the earth's most prolific worms and is the most common earthworm and earthworker in New Zealand. Together with its close relative *Aporrectodea terrestris* (or *longa* which I will use to distinguish it from *Lumbricus terrestris*) and its lesser relative *Aporrectodea chlorotica*, *A. caliginosa* is commonly known as the field worm.

Both forms of *A. caliginosa* are found in paddocks and pastureland, croplands, exotic forests and gardens, and are greatly responsible for breaking down the root-mat under topsoil, making them very desirable topsoil mixers. Huge populations of more than 1.2 million per hectare may be found in top producing pasture, and while they are mostly found with other species *A. caliginosa* is almost always dominant.

Aporrectodea longa (terrestris) is not as common as *A. caliginosa* but is still found throughout much of the country, especially in pastures and cropping soils. It can reach the same high populations as *A. caliginosa* and is very desirable because it works at a lower level than its relative. The distinguishing feature of *A. longa* is its silvery grey iridescence.

Aporrectodea chlorotica is found in many gardens but is particularly active in the Hawke's Bay region. It is extremely useful because of its attraction to wet or waterlogged soils. Although stocky and stout, *A. chlorotica* is a very agile worm and easy to identify because of its greenish colour (although specimens may also be yellow, pink and blue) and the unpleasant odour it leaves on your hands when touched. It coils itself into a tightish knot when disturbed and appears to go into a semi-dormant state.

All species of the genus *Aporrectodea* are earthworkers.

Lumbricus (worm) *terrestris* (earth) is the classic textbook earthworm, and it is often dissected in the classroom and laboratory in the quest for information. *L. terrestris* is the largest of our imported earthworms; it is usually 12–15 cm in length but I have seen many at 20 cm and it can grow up to 30 cm.

L. terrestris is found in many parts of New Zealand, but gardeners and farmers in Auckland and the northern regions should have big populations of these wonderful creatures. It commonly lives in paddocks, forests, lawns, gardens and orchards, and thrives where there is a high concentration of organic material, mineral-rich weeds like dandelion, plantain and dock, or heavy leaf fall.

L. terrestris is a surface feeder but its main feeding ground is more often the upper 45 cm of soil. They frequently burrow to 170–180 cm and have been found in the subsoil at 360–400 cm. Each deep excursion and subsequent return to the surface sees *L. terrestris* bring with it mineral-rich castings which become available to growing plant life.

Its excursions abroad on dewy dark nights give *L. terrestris* popular names like the dewworm or nightcrawler. This is the earthworm eagerly sought after in many parts of the world as fish bait. *L. terrestris* is an earthworker, and my favourite kind of worm.

Lumbricus rubellus is found almost as often as *A. caliginosa*. Although it lives happily in all kinds of situations, it is commonly known as the garden worm, and also as the red worm. *L. rubellus* is a deep red to maroon colour, slightly iridescent, and is very gregarious, often being found with *A. caliginosa, A. longa* and *Octolasium cyaneum*. Occasionally it may be the dominant species in a mixed population.

L. rubellus is interesting because while it does work the upper 5 cm of soil, especially where large amounts of organic litter have been added, it is happy in manure and refuse, and will often enter compost rows or trenches after *E. foetida* has made a start on the job (see page 105). *L. rubellus* is largely responsible for the removal of manure lying on the top of pastures. Earthworms found in cowpats or horse manure are almost always *L. rubellus*. It is both an earthworker and a composter, and where earthworms are cultivated both *L. rubellus* and *E. foetida* will live and breed happily together.

Eisenia foetida, known as the tiger worm because of its red and yellow striped body, and its cousin *Eisenia rosea*, a rich red worm, are common throughout the country, preferring to work in surface areas under luscious rotting vegetation, manure, and in compost. They often wriggle vigorously when handled.

E. foetida can reach huge population levels where cultivated. While its size can reach 8–10 cm, under intensive farming it is closer to 5–7 cm. *E. foetida* are very valuable in refuse schemes and will deal with household waste very easily.

Although *E. foetida* are extremely helpful in forming humus in compost, they will not survive for long transplanted into normal soils unless they are very small and unless special precautions are taken. Though their lives may be shortened when they are transplanted, their dead bodies add nutrients and proteins to the soil.

E. foetida lives close to the surface, rarely going deeper than 15 cm, and thoroughly cultivating the soil around the upper roots of plants. Like *L. rubellus, E. foetida* excretes under the soil surface, making its ammonia-rich castings instantly available to plant and vegetable roots. You can be sure that undesirable castings on lawns, golf courses, bowling greens, cricket pitches or other sportsfields do not belong to either *E. foetida* or *L. rubellus*.

E. foetida is the true composting worm and is happy to be confined and cultivated as long as plenty of food is provided. This worm is probably cultivated more often than all other earthworms combined.

K.E. Lee has recorded that *Octolasium cyaneum* is widespread in New Zealand, but I have only seen a couple of specimens. Its colour is bluey-grey with a bright yellow tail end but it should not be confused with the 'blue' Australian *Perionyx excavatus*. *O. cyaneum* is a fairly thick earthworker which can grow up to 18 cm long, and works up to 15 cm deep. It will extend into isolated pockets of native forest from the surrounding pasture. While it commonly lives in less fertile soils, *O. cyaneum* will live and work in fertile pastureland but only as a minor player in a mixed population.

The major difference between the earthworking species and the composters or cultivated worms is that the earthworkers are better equipped to survive and adapt to the environment, and in dry weather can go deep to find food and moisture. Composters will not survive for long in the soil unless similar conditions to those in which they have been bred — manure, organic material, moisture and oxygen — are supplied. If those needs are continually met, cultivated composters transplanted into soil will live longer than a few weeks, multiply, and carry out soil improvements almost as well as the earthworkers.

What do earthworms need?

Without nature's gifts of sunlight, air, wind and rain, life on planet Earth would cease to be. Earthworms are also one of nature's and evolution's greatest gifts, speeding up the production of humus, and ultimately topsoil, by converting and returning to the soil the detritus and waste products of nature, humans, and all the creatures and organisms which inhabit the earth. Without humus and topsoil, the ability to grow food crops would slow and could indeed stop. It is easy to see then why earthworms are one of our most important tools, to be cherished, admired, protected and encouraged.

For the earthworking species to thrive in their natural habitat, the soil, they have several needs, and where they do not thrive, whether in garden, pasture or cropping soil, make sure you are fulfilling these needs before looking for other reasons.

Sufficient moisture

Without water earthworms cannot survive because they are unable to conserve moisture. They breathe through their bodies and need continual supplies of oxygenated moisture.

Sufficient oxygen

The more dissolved oxygen available in both moisture and soil the healthier the earthworms will be. With plenty of moisture and oxygen the earthworm will be firm to handle and a healthy colour. Oxygen-starved earthworms are pallid and slack. They can do without food for a considerable period, but without water or oxygen they will die.

The right food

Earthworms (especially the composters) will eat almost anything that has lived and died, but for them to become well established in a soil, the organic cycle must provide them with a continual supply of plant debris, as they prefer decaying organic material, dead roots, leaf litter and manure. As the earthworkers eat their way through the moist, oxygenated soil, the nutritional value and quality of the humus they produce is dependent on the quality of the material they eat.

Protection from light

Earthworms, especially the lower-dwelling species, feel pain when exposed to light, especially ultraviolet light. Bare and drying soil without any cover can be very damaging. Applying mulches, cover crops, green manures or areas of hay and straw will provide protection.

The right temperature

Earthworms can handle cold better than heat and can die when the soil temperature rises steeply, unless they retreat deep into the soil and go into diapause, a resting period where they neither eat nor move. This accounts for the absence of earthworms in the topsoil in summer. To a certain extent this can be overcome by putting a cover on, as in protection from light, and by making sure the soil is damp in summer.

The right pH

Although they are very tolerant, earthworms prefer to live in a range in and around neutral, and getting the pH right will sometimes be all that is required to encourage them to thrive. The pH is also important when farming earthworms; when the environment becomes intolerable, the earthworms will leave the beds.

Non-toxic soil

While earthworms prefer not to live in saline or toxic conditions, research suggests that they might be useful in the removal from the soil of toxic substances like cadmium.

— *Earthworms in New Zealand* —

The Reproduction Cycle

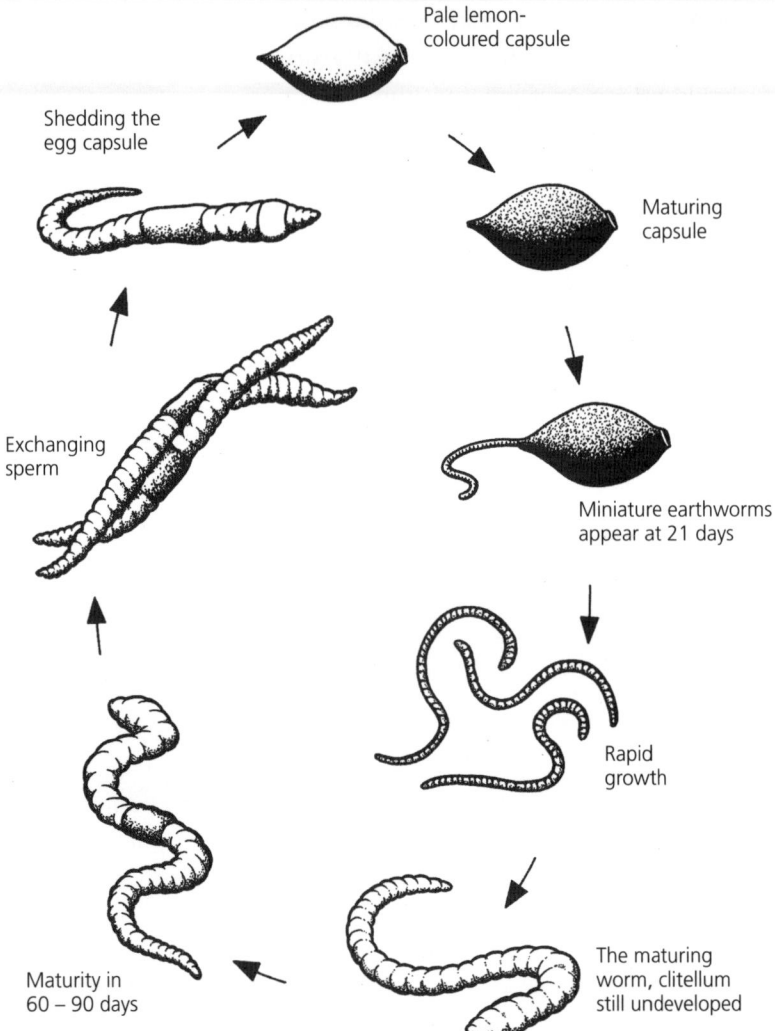

— *What do earthworms need?* —

DIFFERENT RHYTHMS

While the gardener's year might well commence in spring, peak in summer, decline in autumn and remain fallow in winter, earthworms follow a different growth pattern. Their cycle commences in the autumn and declines steeply in the summer, although where composters are cultivated and you control their environment, there should be continual reproduction.

For earthworkers, the hot summer will see many earthworms die after producing their last capsule, while the remainder will be young and immature. The autumn rains stimulate the dormant egg capsules into hatching and this is a time of new life.

The cooler days and nights and the wet weather make them very active, continually feeding on end-of-season organic material, both in and on the soil, and there is heavy casting activity. Forays into new living areas will be made and new burrows built by the *Aporrectodeas*, both to live in and for protection.

This activity continues throughout autumn and winter, and the castings thrown are excellent fertiliser for the spring pasture growth. The young earthworms mature and breed right through to spring. Egg capsules are hatched and many more are laid, and the earthworms' extended families of eggs, very young, immature and mature specimens wax mightily.

Summer finds less activity as the temperature of the soil rises and it dries out. The mature earthworms lay their final capsules and then most die, leaving a young population and unhatched eggs. Some few will retreat into the cooler subsoil regions to aestivate (the summer alternative to winter hibernation). The summer sees a waning of activity, and especially of populations.

In a wet summer the rhythm will change and physical activity will continue. Climatic changes have an enormous effect but the populations can be enhanced throughout the summer by watering or mulching the soil, keeping it cool and moist.

Passing the Time

The nocturnal earthworm's life function is to eat its way through the earth, digesting soil, swallowing dead roots and any and every organic material — protein, carbohydrate, fat, cellulose or lignin, bacterial remains, minute minerals, animal manures and waste; excavating and tunnelling burrows, for both passing through and retiring to; aerating the soil and the subsoil at amazing depths, stimulating growth and better root development of plants and pasture, and making easier the absorption and passage of water into and throughout the soil.

Described by Darwin as one of the strongest animals in nature for its size, an earthworm may move stone particles many times its body-weight. Earthworms move through the soil particles of the earth by constricting and dilating the muscles of their body segments — peristalsis — which in turn provide support for their passage forward. Indeed, it is doubtful whether their lithe and muscular design could be improved to better assist this remarkable performance.

Where the soil is compacted, they will eat their way forward, extracting whatever nutrient is available by grinding, pulverising and digesting it, before excreting the waste product from their bodies as worm casts. It may be waste to earthworms but to the soil it is high in nutrient value and soluble minerals which are readily available to plant life.

If a stone particle is too large to be swallowed the problem is solved by eating around it, although in passing the surface might be

— *Passing the time* —

swiped with mucus — a lick and a promise — so that a future journey might find it more edible. If sufficiently small, the particles will be swallowed and will act as grindstones in the gizzard, again being weathered by the earthworm's digestive acids and alkalis.

While the digestive juices which the earthworm squirts onto the enormous amount of material which passes through its alimentary canal every day are similar to our own stomach juices, earthworms also have special glands in the walls of the oesophagus which secrete calcium. This calciferous fluid seems to provide a neutralising action for the digesting mass.

Nothing is safe from the earthworm's voracious appetite. Kitchen waste, composting organic material, animal manure, almost everything is found agreeable. Dead rats are small potatoes to a bin full of *E. foetida*. After about three weeks all that remain are the slender bones, skull, teeth and mere fragments of skin.

However, like all the creatures of this earth, earthworms, especially *L. terrestris, L. rubellus* and *E. foetida*, have food preferences, enjoying grated carrots and their tops, celery and its flavourful relative lovage, chopped onions but not onion skins, cooked corn husks, chopped comfrey leaves, fruit tree leaves, especially nectarine and peach, and magnolia leaves. I read that they like grated chocolate and found this to be true, but add sweeteners like brown sugar or honey diluted in water, rotting figs and carob to the list of treats.

As you will gather, I have experimented with feeding all sorts of goodies, not only in the worm bins but also at the entrances of *L. terrestris'* burrows and under bricks laid over plastic, where numbers of *A. caliginosa* and *L. rubellus* had made a temporary home.

 An interesting piece of trivia puts the earthworm's function into perspective. While the anterior or front third of the body contains the heart, digestive system organs — crop, gizzard and calciferous glands — and reproductive organs, the remaining two-thirds of the body is almost entirely given over to the intestines. This gives some credence to the comment that the earthworm is nothing more nor less than a long digestive tube.

25

Over a four-week period of nightly feedings and early morning inspections of seven marked burrows, during a damp and dewy early autumn, I enjoyed seeing most of my offerings accepted, although they drew the line at fruit cake soaked in wine. In return *L. terrestris* presented me with huge piles of castings which I collected and watered in directly to my indoor pot plants.

I also kept a daily check on the progress of the large leaves they are adept at pulling down into their burrows, hauling them by the digestible tips rather than the woodier stalk end. Sometimes two or three nights passed before all that remained was a stalk tip.

Forgetting about my special offerings, the last few weeks of late summer and early autumn rain found the earthworms living in my garden, especially *L. terrestris, L. rubellus, A. caliginosa* and *A. trapezoides*, coming to the surface at night to feed on leaves and other organic litter.

By day their previous night's forays and excursions were apparent by the castings they left. During the day all is quiet on the surface, while in their subterranean world they carry out further excavations and build more tunnels. Their secretive lives might be described as furtive unless you accept that even early morning light can hurt them, and ultraviolet light and bright sunlight are killers. Yes, they do feel pain, even though their nervous system is rudimentary.

I know you can't make friends with or pets of earthworms, but my past and recent autumn experiences have left me with the greatest admiration for these small and clever denizens of the dark, especially *L. terrestris*.

Care needed

Earthworms need to take careful precautions against drying out. They collect oxygen through their outer skin, which must remain moist to act as an efficient respirator. This is one of the reasons why few earthworms are found in the upper and drier soil surface in the summer. Those that survive high summer heat and extreme dryness may have retreated a metre or more down into the subsoil to find a moister and kinder environment. If you have only looked for earthworms in your garden during the summer months, this may be one of the reasons why you have found few.

Smaller and immature worms which have remained in the top 15 cm of soil during the summer (usually *A. caliginosa*, *A. chlorotica* or *L. rubellus*) will often coil themselves into a tight knot inside a mucus-lined chamber of compact earth where they aestivate until the rain again softens the soil. Thoughtful gardeners who ensure that the ground is watered or who apply mulch covers will find that the earthworms in their gardens will continue to survive and thrive in summer.

Where the available organic material encourages the spread of earthworm populations *A. caliginosa*, which do not care for cramped and crowded conditions, will migrate during spring rain. Ten worms in a 30 cm by 10 cm piece of turf might be called overcrowding, and while *E. foetida* is happy to cram, *A. caliginosa* seems to need more space and privacy.

However, any worm found abroad after sunrise is in danger of paralysis from ultraviolet light and unless cover — mulch, leaf litter, old sacking, corrugated iron, long damp grass — is rapidly found, they are unable to burrow quickly enough to escape. After heavy rain, the lethargic earthworms you see on the roads or in gutters are suffering from exposure to light. Unless they have been too much exposed, you may save them by gathering them up and placing them in shade or dark, covering them with moist paper or sacking until they recover and go about their peripatetic business.

While evolution and adaptation now make the earthworm a land creature, worms can live in lakes, ponds or streams for some time as long as plenty of oxygen is available. Worms not only come to the surface after heavy rain to avoid drowning, but also because the amount and pressure of rainwater in the burrows decreases the amount of oxygen available. They also take advantage of slippery wet conditions to migrate to greener and more appetising pastures and to spread their colonies.

How do they mate?

Earthworms are hermaphrodites, but almost all species must mate with another mature worm before they can perform both the male and female functions for which they are equipped. In this remarkable process two lots of semen are exchanged, with which each worm then fertilises its own eggs.

They are ready to breed when the clitellum — the sign of maturity approximately one-third back from the mouth end — thickens, normally after 60 to 90 days.

Head to tail, the two mature worms twine around each other until their clitella are brought into contact. Once the worms are vitally positioned sperm is undulated and exchanged into the storage sacs, and the two then separate. This is a slow, balletic performance — which seems especially slow if you are watching. The complete process is not accomplished for over 24 hours, longer with some varieties, until mucus, secreted over the clitellum in a band or collar, slides forward along the body forcing the sperm and egg storage pores into contact. The number of worms in each capsule depends upon the speed at which the band has passed over the egg sacs, but can be as many as twenty worms (for *E. foetida*) although it is usually around four to six, again depending on the species. The worm slips its body backwards until the collar slides off the head end, then the collar shrinks to form a pale, lemon-coloured oval cocoon or capsule.

The tiny teardrop capsules, from 2–5 mm across depending on the species, are sometimes mistaken for slow-release fertiliser. The capsules lie in the soil or breeding bin for from two weeks to six months, depending on the variety, temperature and moisture, or other factors (see page 98). Capsules can even survive under water. Once hatched, each tiny, perfectly formed and self-sufficient earthworm is able to begin its life's work.

Within three to four months each worm is able to breed, although full maturity is not reached for around 12 months. Mating can occur again and again over the breeding season. An active breeding composter can produce approximately 50 to 60 capsules

— *Passing the time* —

per year, and taking an average of 4 per cycle, that is 200 young earthworms. Again, the young worms themselves become breeders within three to four months, resulting in a rapid pyramiding of production within the year.

While the mating arrangements are similar for all species, the proclivities of some, like *L. terrestris*, must be accounted for. Firstly, getting it on for *L. terrestris* is limited to dewy, calm autumn or winter nights or dull, very early mornings when the moist soil has been softened by plenty of rain.

Secondly, and unlike many of his/her confreres, *L. terrestris* mates on the surface, while never quite leaving home. This is accomplished by two worms from adjacent burrows — which must be quite close together for matters to advance — bringing their forward segments together while leaving their rear ends safe and secure in their respective burrows. Congress proceeds and may take several hours, and while rain won't separate them, disturbances like sudden light, vibration or nosey parkers like me make them disengage smartly in a retreat so hasty you wonder whether you really saw what you thought you saw. Talk about coitus interruptus!

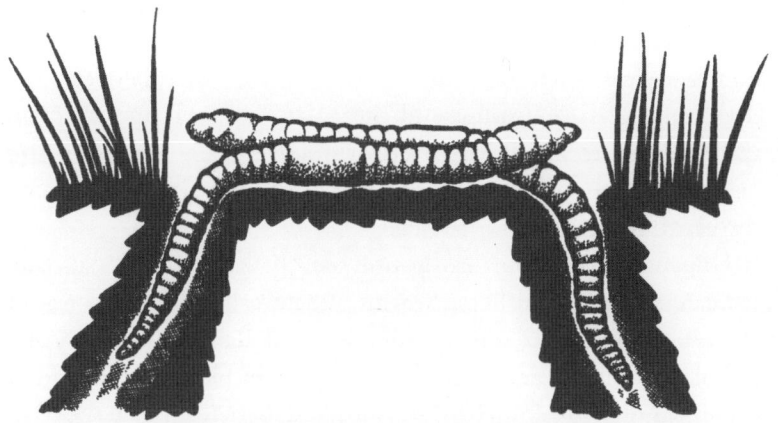

Lumbricus terrestis mating across adjacent burrows

Soil — the living environment

Most of us have little knowledge of what the soil can reveal, but the geological history and evidence of occupation by animals and humans can often be gathered simply by digging holes in the earth and looking at the soil profile and structure.

Where clean cuts of the profile are examined, as in post or tree holes, drain trenches, soak pits, road cuttings or building excavations, much can be learnt about soil composition — whether clay, loam, sandstone or volcanic — and its present and previous tenants.

By looking carefully you will see the extent of topsoil layers, where earthworms have made their passage through the soil, where they have aestivated, and where they have cast residue from their bodies — easily seen in burrows by the difference between the dark, mineral-rich castings and the paler wall surround. You can trace the species which have lived, or still live, in the soil by the size of their tunnels and the direction these may be following through the earth, vertically or horizontally.

Depending on your excavation depth, large tunnels usually indicate larger subsoil-living worms. Whatever size, the presence of burrows means better soil aeration, the possibility of more moisture available for plants, deeper and easier access for plant roots to gather mineral nutrients from the subsoil, and benefits from the rich castings left by earthworms as they dive.

Breaking apart the soil removed from the hole will reveal further secrets. Where burrows end in slightly bigger, rounded chambers or cells and are lined with a delicate shiny film of dried mucus, you can assume that a worm has spent much of the summer aestivating, withdrawing from the heat and lack of moisture. Smaller chambers might enclose egg capsules waiting for winter rains to reactivate them.

Look to the soil profile again for further information. Unless you are unlucky enough to have had the topsoil removed and literally sold out from under your feet, the top 200–300 mm of soil is where most of the action is. The crumblier layer should contain not only earthworms but a proportion of decayed and decaying organic matter (humus) and millions of living and dying organisms and bacteria on which earthworms feed and from which plant roots draw nourishment.

Here too you will find out what kind of soil you have, whether it might be described as zonal, intrazonal or azonal, light or heavy, mature or immature, weathered or organic, sandy, clay, volcanic, silt or loam.

The second layer is the subsoil, which may continue for some metres into the earth and which is being constantly formed either by the decaying lowest layer or horizon in mature soils, or still being laid down in immature soils by other methods such as earthquakes, erosion, flooding, wind deposits, or other natural means.

The third layer or lowest horizon is that most ancient section of the planet Earth, the underlying rock bottom, absolute bedrock.

SOIL CHARACTERISTICS

So what are the differing characteristics of soil? What is the best kind to have? Can earthworms help change the soil's characteristics, even *improve* the soil?

Clay soils are sticky and heavy, which makes them difficult to cultivate, but they are full of nutritious minerals. Slow, sometimes impossible to drain, they contain less oxygen and fewer aerating tunnels because the soil particles stick together. The texture of clay soil may be improved by adding quantities of organic material and additives like gypsum which will break down the clay.

Sandy soils are easier to dig and cultivate, and they drain more easily than clay, but their organic content is quickly used up and their light nature allows nutrients and added lime to be washed away easily. Sandy soils need frequent liming and heavy applications of compost or organic material to help keep the soil particles together.

River **silts** are fine and fertile and hold moisture easily, but their light structure breaks down very quickly, sometimes causing erosion. Silts need lashings of compost and other organic material which breaks down slowly and will help bind the particles together.

Loam is the queen of soils, a desirable rich and fertile product which carries the good qualities of sand and clay. Loam contains a good ratio of decaying organic material or humus, and continually adding compost will keep loam fertile.

Traditional thinking and practice suggests that the best soil to produce prolific crops has three basic characteristics: it must be able to hold moisture, especially during the dry season; have sufficient friability, oxygen and space for root development, and contain sufficient nutrients for growing plants.

Plants thrive where the soil structure is good and the fertility high, and it is likely to remain that way if, when the plants are harvested, their organic remains are allowed to decay into humus and stimulate the micro-organisms in healthy living soil into abundant life. When earthworms are present they help transform and process the rich minerals and organic matter into chemical building blocks, encouraging new plants to thrive.

The physical and fibrous bulk of humus helps to break down solid soil particles, which not only makes it easier for water to drain

---

Farmers, cropgrowers, market and domestic gardeners can help increase the natural but slow humus build-up by adding plenty of bulky organic material and compost to enhance the natural plant material. Stable muck, cowshed manure, rotting hay, pine needles and other mulches can all be added to the top of the soil and allowed to break down slowly. Any soil type will appreciate regular helpings of humus.

through the soil but also aids moisture retention. Broken-down soil particles help air to penetrate and oxygenate plant roots and the hair-like root system.

Humus and bulky materials like hay, straw and manures are great for the soil's physical composition because they take time to decompose and combine with soil particles. They increase the soil's ability to retain plant food and moisture. The best soil structure encourages strenuous root growth so plants can contend with occasional hardship.

Sadly, few of the world's natural soils fall into the 'loam' category any longer, as a result of erosion, wholesale forest removal, overcropping, and a host of other man-made ills. New Zealand has its share of loams but some of our soils are deficient in one or other of the basic requirements, so farmers and other soil workers have to correct the deficiencies or else adopt practices which will help increase the soil's fertility.

Where moisture levels are inadequate, adding water and conserving moisture is essential, but this added water must run into, not run off, the ground. When the soil lacks oxygen, as in clay, drainage must be improved and the clay particles broken down to increase the space between them. Where soil tests show that specific nutrients are missing, animal manures, organic fertilisers or supplements must be added, or nitrogen-rich crops like legumes can be grown.

Many measures taken by gardeners and farmers to correct deficiencies might be unnecessary if we added another basic requirement to our list right at the beginning. You've guessed it! Our friends the earthworms, the best and cheapest earthworker available.

In his North American study, 'What Every Gardener Should Know About Earthworms', soil scientist Dr Henry Hopp says: 'Earthworm activity is not one of the three basic requirements for plant growth. Rather it comes into the category of factors which can be used to correct deficiencies in these basic requirements.' But Dr Hopp then concludes, '. . . on some soils it is difficult to find other means of doing those things which are normally done by earthworms.'

I believe that earthworms should be considered a *basic* requirement to soil fertility and health, their presence ensuring higher crop yields and better pasture growth.

Earthworms — the great transformers

Topsoil is essential for our continued existence. Concentrated in a small outer layer of the earth, its fertility is constantly depleted and must be renewed. Nature, using every tool at her disposal, slowly and incessantly recycles the organic waste products of all animal life, from microbe to man, transforming them into rich humus to be incorporated in the topsoil and reused in the continuum of life and death. It is a remarkable process, taking from 500 to 1,000 years to build 25 mm of topsoil.

Nature's processes can be helped where large and mixed earthworm populations can be encouraged. Surface litter species start by breaking down organic litter and manure and incorporating it into the top 5 cm of soil. Topsoil species continue the transition by combining organic material and the broken down manure into humus, and finally the subsoil species complete the transformation by mixing the humus with subsoil minerals.

Earthworm populations

While earthworms have a penchant for soils in the neutral range and will migrate to those which originate from limestone, they may be enticed into soils rich in organic materials. Soil texture will also influence their peregrinations, and their preference for clay over sandy soils, which have little density, is fortunate. Even so, they will avoid clay which is waterlogged because it is low in oxygen.

Mineral-rich clay may be, but without heavy additions of bulky organics or gypsum, or earthworms to break down and work through the packed soil particles, it may be too compressed for crop growth.

Earthworms avoid stony soils and they do not like pumice soils. However, if a suitable and hospitable microclimate encourages them to exist even within such an inhospitable area, they will colonise.

With a very few exceptions, they will converge on areas high in nitrogen-rich organic material, because earthworms need huge quantities of this material to convert into protein, that compound which makes up the greater part of their bodies' dry weight. Assuming that their other demands for water, warmth, soil pH and texture have been met, the lack of nitrogen-rich material can sometimes be the main reason for any limited populations.

Let's look at that in a different way. The earthworm populations in New Zealand pine forests, for example, while establishing themselves at reasonable levels, will be quite different from those in deciduous forests where the normal autumn leaf fall encourages high earthworm activity. But in an excellent season of moderate temperatures and high rainfall, the *quality* of leaves dropped might be higher than in lack-lustre years, supplying better food and encouraging the self-limiting population to rise. Again, as the trees grow bigger there will be *higher* leaf drop, also encouraging an increase. Conversely, a bad year might see a decrease in the population.

So the earthworm population is continually adjusted not only by the supply of leaves but also by the nitrogenous content of their

Because the European earthworm species in New Zealand are mainly topsoil dwellers that feed on dead roots and the leaf litter from pasture, they dominate the indigenous species in our pastoral economy. It can be fairly said that although soil differences may influence the natural spread of the European lumbricids, their populations are affected far more by the farming and conservation methods used than by soil type. However, where even limited populations exist within a given area or region, their migration to new living quarters will be affected both by the food available and by their soil preferences.

food. This is as true for the populations living in home gardens, pastures and croplands. Earthworm populations will only rise when extra food in the form of manures, organic materials, compost and mulches is regularly added to the living environment. The added benefit is an increase in the soil's nutrient value and structure.

How mixed populations help below the ground

The ideal human community benefits from a mixture of peoples drawn from different ethnic and sociological backgrounds, with each person contributing his or her best to the society. An ideal earthworm population is no different. Remember that the soil is the earthworm's home, where different colonies live and get on together, work, breed, shift houses, live out their lives.

An earthworm colony may have similar problems with the physical environment to some of us — too hot, too cold, too wet, too dry, insufficient food, crowded living conditions, aggressive predators, sudden death.

An ideal earthworm population would be mixed because the different species all work at different levels and burrow at different depths. Species found closer to the surface are usually redder in colour, because there is more oxygen available, and they devour more organic material, again because it is available. The bigger subsoil species are paler because less oxygen is available, and they swallow a higher proportion of soil in an adaptation to living conditions where organic food is minimal.

Depending on the population mixture, earthworm burrows — like subterranean mining highways — can be major or minor, highway or access, narrow or wide (1 mm up to 10 mm — rarely 20 mm, in the case of *S. gigantea*), can cross each other, be vertical or horizontal, start at the surface and continue into the soil for over two metres or more. The delicate film lining the burrows will be rich in calcium carbonate, iron, manganese or other minerals depending on availability and the depths at which the burrows have been tunnelled.

The result of all this excavating, tunnelling and casting activity in

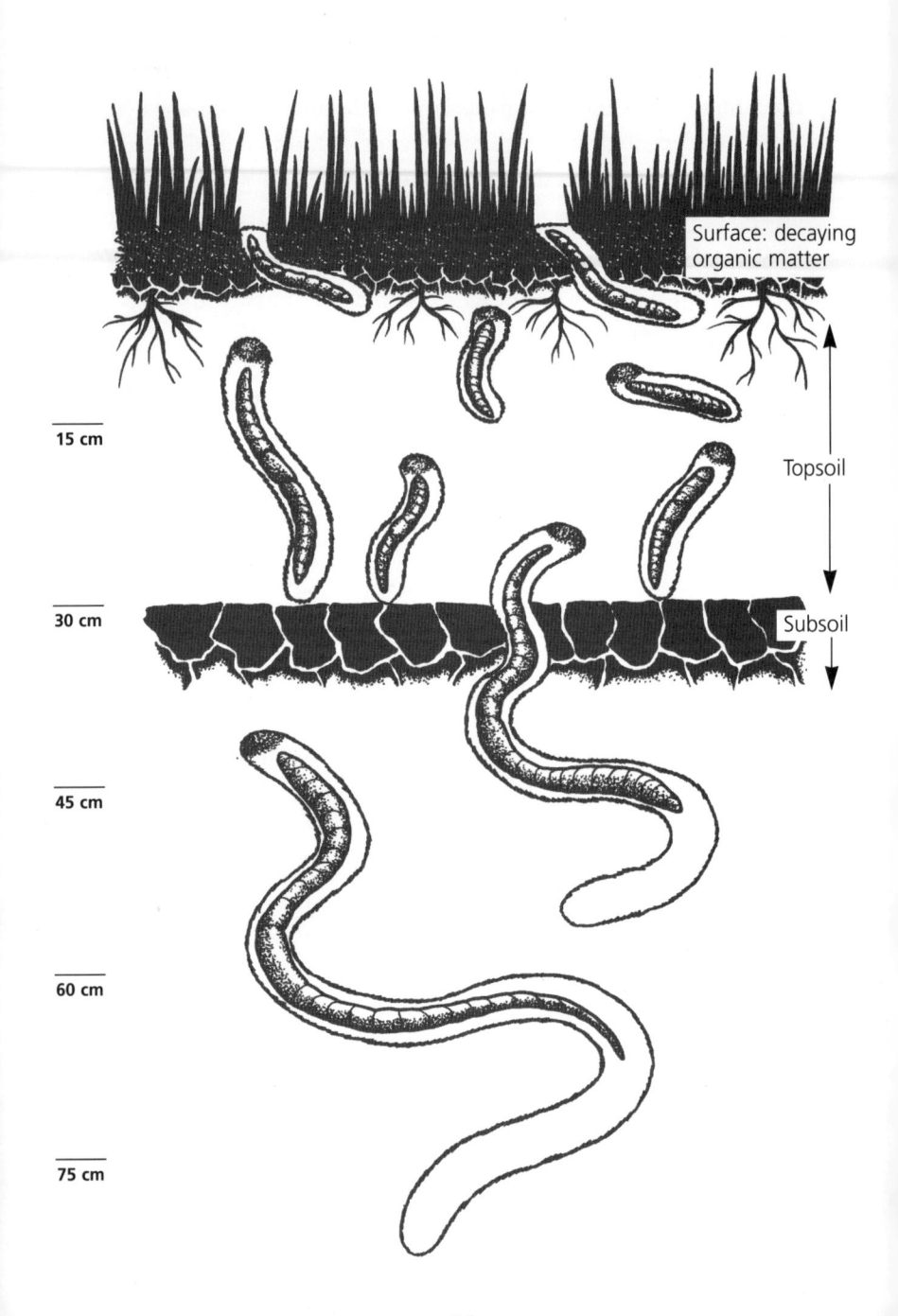

— *Earthworms in New Zealand* —

the earthworms' world under our feet is rich and various, and responsible for important changes in the soil environment. For example, the soil aeration can increase, in extreme situations by as much as 60 percent, with the moister air in this network of burrows encouraging a bigger plant root mass to develop, in turn attracting increased moisture. Rainwater is able to penetrate further, increasing the soil porosity and being absorbed by the mineral-rich castings in the burrows, instead of running off or sitting on the surface of the soil.

As long as continual supplies of food are made available the number of burrows can extend until the mineral-rich organic soil resembles a giant sponge holding the life-giving moisture in place. This earthworm environment is warmer in winter and cooler in summer, and results in an earlier growth start for plants and a longer growing season.

How mixed populations help on the soil surface

While the water absorbancy of soil is greatly improved by earthworm burrows, their activities also influence what happens on the surface. Where there are no earthworms, prolonged dry or wet weather may encourage silt and clay soils to compact and much of the water will run off the surface instead of entering it. Sometimes, even where there is adequate rainfall plants and crops may suffer, unless earthworms have helped work the soil and mulches have been applied.

A decent earthworm population working for even a month will improve the soil structure and encourage water to enter the soil. Fine sandy soils with little cover and structure encourage run-off and it is important to lay mulches so that worms can work under cover, especially in the summer, or to incorporate compost or humus into the soil so that worms will make the topsoil layer more friable and allow water to penetrate faster.

In a vegetable patch it is a good idea to cut vegetables like lettuces off at ground level, leaving the roots in the ground, and dig the tops of carrots or beets back into the soil straightaway. In the flower garden hoe the tops off any young weeds and turn them into the soil. The earthworms will be grateful and commence work within a short period of wilting and decomposition.

There is often a connection between the rate of water absorption and the number of earthworms. Where there are plenty of worms the soil will absorb water pretty quickly and there is little danger of run-off and subsequent erosion. Conversely where there are few earthworms the absorption rate will be slower with the likelihood of erosion higher. Eroded soil not only has a lower organic content but the likelihood of mineral washout is increased. Remember that erosion does not happen unless there is excessive water run-off, and a substantial earthworm population will increase not only the water absorbancy of soil but also penetration of the topsoil layer.

Other helpful creatures

Of course earthworms don't do it all on their own, and their presence in soil seems to stimulate an increase in the microscopic life of the soil, which in fertile pastureland topsoil already contains tonnes of micro-organisms per hectare.

Let's take another look at the earthworm's main function in life: to eat, break down and excrete dead roots, soil particles, including dead micro-organisms, surface organic litter and manure — a potpourri of organic material. In a final contribution, the earthworm's dead body adds protein and minerals to the biomass.

However, much of the swallowed food, although broken down, is excreted before its nutritional value has been exhausted. It is this undigested remnant of the excreted humus, containing millions of microbes which have lived and multiplied in the worm's gut, that stimulates the activity of the soil microfauna into a bacterial level

Earthworms are not a modish fad of the late twentieth century. Thousands of earthworm fanciers have appreciated the small creatures since the Egyptians revered them and made their removal from the rich river silt of the great Nile Valley a life-losing offence.

---

which can be many times higher than the level in other soils. These micro-organisms — fungi, algae, moulds — converge on the castings and gorge on the remnant nutrients, converting it into even finer humus, distributing it throughout the soil horizons, increasing the nutrients and therefore the soil fertility.

Earthworm vermicast! Is it different?

Plenty of research points to castings, or vermicast, being superior to unprocessed soil. As the swallowed soil passes through the earthworm it encounters digestive juices and chemicals which enable the minerals in the soil to be surrendered more readily. Soil which houses earthworms is also superior because a high earthworm population will mix its castings with the topsoil layers so well that it becomes impossible to tell one from t'other, and I can vouch for that.

Generally speaking, the top layers of soil contain more nitrogen and phosphorus than the subsoil layers, which carry other important plant food minerals. Where continual cropping, even home gardening, is carried out without any organic material or compost being added, the nitrogen and phosphorus content in the topsoil will eventually degrade, until it equals the lower subsoil percentages.

Gardeners have always known that soil fertility can be improved by mixing the two soils, hence the traditional and back-breaking method of double trenching. But if you bring subsoils to the surface, especially from lower than 45 cm, it will need weathering for some time before being mixed sparingly with the top layers, otherwise, instead of the fertility being increased, it may well be reduced.

Having a large mixed population of earthworms will make a huge improvement in mixing the subsoil and topsoil layers. It is fairly clear that any 'weathering' of the soil is undergone during its journey through the alimentary canals of the earthworms. But they do not just swallow the subsoil, bring it to the surface and dump it. Further passages through the earthworms see it mixed with the topsoil to a uniform layer.

Huge earthworm populations can push tonnes of soil through their systems annually, and deliver it either directly to the roots of plants or to the surface of the soil, speeding up nature's work by centuries. Too much research has been done and too much soil has been created by the earthworms for any but the most sceptical to doubt it.

Maybe the mental picture of tonnes of soil is too great for you to contemplate. Try and visualise the humus-making, soil-building earthworms making soil in a small flowerpot, a citrus barrel, a no-dig above-the-soil garden, in the glasshouse, munching your kitchen waste on the balcony of your tenth-storey inner city apartment, revitalising an old orchard, converting huge piles of organic waste in landfills, reducing food processing wastes in food factories, in composting toilets, or finally on a huge scale in pastureland.

Remember, however, that nought is made from nought and that this new soil cannot be created without the base material to work with, and without huge numbers of earthworms to do a Rumplestiltskin.

Remember also that where temperature, moisture and pH make the environment hospitable, the only limiting factors to increasing the number of earthworms by thousandfolds are the amounts of available food, the use of inorganic fertilisers and toxic chemicals, and farming methods that are harmful to worms.

Every possible form of organic material can be used as worm food: vegetation, manures, soil waste, kitchen and household waste,

---

Here's a useful experiment to try. Layer a 40-cm-deep box or crate with equal parts of deeper soil (at least a spade depth), crumbly manure and topsoil. Be sure, for your future observation, that your layers are even and obvious. Dampen thoroughly and introduce 50 *A. caliginosa* or *L. terrestris*. If you can't find them, add 500–1,000 *E. foetida* and *L. rubellus*. Leave the box for at least six weeks, making sure it is continually moist. Be delighted when you see the mixture turned into crumbly even-textured soil.

---

garden, orchard and farm waste, all kinds of litter; anything that has lived and died is earthworm food at some stage in the cycle of deterioration. And if it's earthworm fodder, that means an increase in earthworms and an increase in humus and fine topsoil.

More recent research figures are doubtless available, but I'd like to repeat those I quoted when I first wrote about worms in *Earthworms Unlimited*.

Experiments at the Connecticut Agricultural Station have shown that earthworm castings contain approximately *five* times more available nitrogen, *seven* times more available phosphorus, *three* times more exchangeable magnesium, *one-and-a-half* times more calcium and *eleven* times more available potassium than ordinary topsoil.

COLLECTING EARTHWORMS

During the 1995 morris dance festival in the Auckland Domain, thousands of earthworms came to the surface and were killed by the many stamping feet. Ironically, this old-time fertility ritual is very bad news for earthworms unless kind people remove the inert worms. Twanging and vibrating a garden or pitch fork driven into hard ground will also disturb earthworms, but will not bring them all to the surface.

There are other ways to collect earthworms for worm beds, fishing or for transplanting into pasture or gardens. Dig for them on damp spring or autumn days, especially if you are after *L. terrestris*, or look for *A. caliginosa* and *L. rubellus* in early morning light after heavy rain, when many may be found. Providing you supply them with the food and lodgings they need they will be happy to live

Try and visualise earthworms, not as single rather helpless individuals, or even in units of 500, but as powerful stock units encompassing thousands or millions of earthworms, as efficient a social community as you could hope to find, an investment worth every bit as much as your dairy herd, your expensive emus, or your next New Zealand Cup winner. The only difference is that your earthworm stock work for you beneath the surface of the earth.

with and work for you. Look in the bottoms and sides of drains, under piles of grass or hay, in weed-covered areas of the garden or in damp sections and paddocks.

Although I have not used either of the following two methods, a 0.2 percent solution of formalin or potassium permanganate (Condy's crystals) poured over the ground or lawn will bring a number to the surface. So will a squirt of detergent in a bucket of water. If you try this, gather the worms up quickly and wash them in a bucket of water to help them recover. You may still have some casualties. Of course if you wish to reduce the earthworm population living and casting on your lawn you will not be interested in rinsing the worms. Genocide!

PART II

New Zealand as an Earthworm-Friendly Environment

Is it possible to engender the philosophy of an entire country as an earthworm-friendly environment, when the country has a market-driven economy?

The answer is probably yes, if we use the market-driven philosophy to advance the cause, because despite New Zealand's diverse new products and markets, and to the surprise of many, we are still very dependent on our traditional agricultural products. Farmers and workers in agriculture and, increasingly, horticulture must resist any attempts to downgrade their importance to the economy, and strive for international recognition of New Zealand as a giant larder, the environmentally friendly green country with a cornucopia of high-health, chemical-free, fresh produce.

Of course that 'green' assertion might encourage a hollow laugh from some as long as we continue to use huge quantities of herbicides and pesticides, even when their use is justified as a condition of entry for produce being exported to other countries. But the rising clamour from many parts of the world for organically grown produce is the market-driven signal that we should revise our thinking, clean up our act and wholeheartedly embrace the principles of organic farming. By responding to consumer demand we can accentuate the positive and reap the benefits of a clean green image.

One of the keys to this potential success is the humble

earthworm. We can all do our bit by fostering earthworm-friendly environments in gardens and pastures of all sizes; the small creatures will then help us prove that the soil really is richer and the grass really is greener and thicker down here in the South Pacific. Huge congregations of earthworms in backyard gardens from the far north to the deep south, in small holdings and large spreads, in orchards, market gardens and forests, will encourage and maintain soil fertility. And farmed earthworms will devour organic waste and produce tonnes of vermicast to spread on pasture and cropland, promoting soil health and good structure.

As the world becomes more and more polluted, the green forests on the rest of the planet become depleted, and the world's population continues to increase, we can truly say that we care for our environment and back it up with facts. Well, that's the dream, but it's a dream that people of every persuasion — greenies, alternative lifestylers, farmers, gardeners, as well as economists — can share.

In the following chapters we'll take a look at compost making, and how in utilising and adapting the compost process we can encourage earthworms in backyard gardens, farms, croplands and orchards, and under intensive cultivation.

Speeding up the transformation

Most people know that the sun's energy helps plants grow, providing the wherewithal by activating the chlorophyll in leaves, which synthesises the air's carbon dioxide and the soil's water to make sugars and starches.

Oxygen, combined chemically with other trace elements, is taken up by the roots, while decaying organic matter, mulches and compost provide some of the carbon dioxide needed by plants and help the oxygen supply by opening up, draining and aerating the soil.

Earthworms and their mini compatriots the micro-organisms are essential ingredients in the soil fertility mix, because they speed up the production of compost and humus and increase its quality. Because compost and humus are essential to vigorous and healthy soil production, whether in a pocket handkerchief vegetable garden or on a 100-hectare farm, we need some understanding of what happens in the composting process, and a swift, simple lesson in compost making. The principles are the same whether you are making small quantities in gardens or huge amounts on farms.

Compost

Compost is made from the organic and biodegradable waste products of households, gardens, farms, forests and seashore. It is produced by millions upon millions of micro-organisms too small to be seen — bacteria, fungi, algae, actinomycetes and enzymes — and thousands upon thousands of macro-organisms — mites, nematodes, slugs, earthworms, centipedes, earwigs and other insects — as well as sunlight, air, moisture and time.

Where plenty of delicious food is available and the compost pile has been arranged in a seductive manner, the micro populations multiply rapidly, increasing the rate of decomposition and producing intense heat. In a very hot heap the micro-organisms' work slows once the oxygen supply decreases, and the heap needs turning to introduce more air and rev up the rate of decomposition.

Once the softer materials have been attacked and subdued the heavier material, cellulose and lignin, comes under scrutiny, and because this requires more work and energy, the heap cools down. At this stage the macro-organisms, bugs, earthworms and so on, which have been waiting in the wings, make a stealthy occupation and continue the work.

Every one of the micro-organisms has its own special use and function, and the more varied the population the better. Without the micro-organisms there would be little decomposition, leaving the nutrients inert, locked away in the organic material. Without the micro-organisms there would be no compost, so they need encouragement to multiply in the compost heap, in the form of the things they need besides oxygen and moisture — sources of *energy*, *nitrogen* and *vitamins*. While the material with which you build your compost pile will probably contain the micro-organisms' requirements, it is worthwhile being specific about these needs.

The *energy* requirement can be met by a simple sugar, be it cellulose — plant outer coverings — or lignin — a wood fibre component. The *nitrogen* source can be found in the protein of any of the natural activators, like blood and bone, manures, loamy soil, fish waste, ground hoof or horn. The *vitamin* requirement is easiest

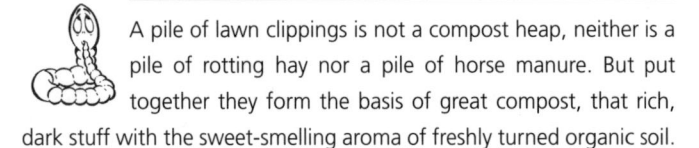

A pile of lawn clippings is not a compost heap, neither is a pile of rotting hay nor a pile of horse manure. But put together they form the basis of great compost, that rich, dark stuff with the sweet-smelling aroma of freshly turned organic soil.

---

to fill because vitamins are found in plant and animal tissue.

While the composting pile is intensely hot, medium temperature actinomycetes, part bacteria and part fungus, and cooler temperature fungi are working on the outer edges, beginning to break down the tough cellulose and lignin. Once the pile has cooled completely they move in holus bolus, and after considerable occupation their presence can be detected by a greyish cobwebby look and a pleasant earthy smell in the heap.

The macro-organisms — mites, nematodes, insects and earthworms — also move in once the pile has cooled, and they help chew, digest, tunnel, burrow and mix all the compostable material together.

While the earthworms consume and digest almost all the organic matter, they seem to have a sympathetic relationship with bacteria; while each can live well separately, the partnership has mutual benefits. Earthworms digest food for the bacteria, the bacteria digest food for the earthworms, and once the bacteria die, they too become earthworm food. Finally, the dead and decomposing bodies of all the macro-organisms, along with the minuscule remains of bacteria, add nitrogen and protein to the compost.

When compost piles get insufficient oxygen, aerobic bacteria cannot survive and are replaced by anaerobic bacteria. Sufficient quantities of oxygen and carbon dioxide can neither pass in nor pass out. The decomposing process slows down and the anaerobes produce organic acids and smelly ammonia-like substances which tell you that, among other things, the pH is too low. Turning the heap to introduce air and adding lime or any of the substances which raise the pH, such as ground pipi or oyster shell, wood ashes, dolomite or bone meal, will neutralise the acids and raise the pH.

MAKING A COMPOST PILE

Earthworms, bacteria, fungi et al. already lurk within your garden, waiting for goodies to gorge upon, and the sooner you come to grips with the concept of *you helping nature help you*, the easier the composting process will be for you to understand.

All organic materials are compostable and you will make great compost if you follow three simple requirements: plenty of air, adequate moisture, and varied organic material. If you fulfil those three requirements, the micro-organisms will start working and reproducing and your compost heap will operate efficiently.

Ideally the compost area should be accessible, open to some sunlight and not in the draughtiest corner of the section. Have all of your compostable material on hand and collect as many different ingredients as you can get hold of. It may be necessary to stockpile materials before you start building your pile, otherwise the heating process may take longer.

Break, chop, chip or grind everything as small as you can manage. Breaking warms you up for the chopping, which reduces bulk, and bruises and tears the tough skin on vegetable material. Grinding exposes more surface area and breaks down plant tissue, especially cellulose. Use your rotary mower, machete, clippers or an organic matter grinder if you have access to one. Using the kitchen whizz is going a bit far. If possible mix and blend the various materials as you chop, chip and grind. Doing this helps the micro-organisms attack from all sides.

Loosen the soil to a depth of about 10 cm. Lay down a thick layer of coarse organic material like hedge clippings, straw or hay to encourage aeration, but not so thickly as to raise the pile too far off the ground, which will initially discourage heat, and later earthworms. A good rule of thumb is to avoid making any layer of material more than 15–25 cm thick, although I always place a decent layer (30–40 cm) of horse or sheep manure next to the first layer. Commercially prepared sheep pellets are excellent if you can't get fresh manure and need not be laid so heavily.

Build the pile alternating green layers of fresh material with dry layers of weathered material like manure or hay, and absorbent thin layers like soil or shredded paper with wet layers like grass clippings or sloppy kitchen waste (sprinkled with lime). A basic rule to follow is two parts of vegetable matter to one part animal manure. As you build the heap, toss the individual layers as much as possible,

— *Speeding up the transformation* —

allowing air to enter. Although you don't need to exercise care while doing this, think about how and why you fold dry ingredients into beaten eggs and sugar when making spongecake.

With the hose on a fine mist, sprinkle water after every few layers until the pile is like a wrung out sponge. A damp pile is very important, but too much moisture, say 60 percent or more, may produce a soggy, smelly, anaerobic mess. However, if the moisture content is lower than 40 percent, the organic material will not decompose fast enough. Lots of ants around the pile are usually a sign that it is too dry. Do a Goldilocks until you get it just right.

Repeat the layering process as often as necessary to use all the material, but don't make the pile too big. Better to make two piles than one enormous unturnable mass, unless you're on a farm using mechanical help. Somewhere between 1.5 and 2 metres is about right. A heavy layer of straw or hay to save heat loss and avoid leaching by rain can be used on top of and around the pile. But be easy about this, as you should be about the materials you're using.

The heap layers can easily be changed. Leave out the soil, or the lime, or both. If no manure of any kind is available, replace the bulk with a combination of shredded newspaper, cardboard or documents, which can be bought by the bale. Use another activator or starter, like dried blood, fish waste, ground hoof or horn, meat scraps or bone meal. What the activator is providing is a nitrogen-protein source which will encourage and feed the micro-organisms.

Top with a waterproof cover if you like. I avoid covering the pile until the weather gets very cold and wet, and then I use either old carpet, hessian, or black polythene (sometimes I forget). An old tarpaulin would be good. As the pile shrinks — anywhere from 20 to 60 percent depending on the materials used — you can add new layers, but only add material while the working model still has a couple of weeks to go. (Better to start a new heap.) Usually, finished compost will weigh approximately half to three-quarters the weight of the original material. While I sometimes forget to cover the working heap I *always* cover the finished compost.

You will have a good idea about what supplies to use: lawn and hedge clippings, weeds, hay and any type of straw, manures of any kind including dog waste and cat litter, any garden waste, old or spent soil, wood ash, shredded paper and cardboard, kitchen waste. On the farm a large proportion of the heap can be animal manure as long as a good portion of hay or straw is added as well.

But think about all the other things you can use. House waste, for example, includes vacuum cleaner dust, dead houseplants, dog and human hair, feathers, cotton, silk and wool waste, fine and ground shells, and coffee grounds; then there's spent hops, sawdust, seaweed, pine needles, peat moss, leaves (see leaf mould), or air-dried sewer sludge (high in nitrogen). Cooked corn cobs are good because earthworms love to eat out the middle and breed inside them. If you are using seedy weeds you will need manure or other nitrogen-rich material to generate heat and kill the seeds.

Turning the pile is a bind, especially if you've made the heap too big, but doing it occasionally helps it decompose faster. Don't turn it too often. Rely on the heat being generated to tell you when it needs turning. If it has cooled it may be time for a turn. Frankly I only ever turn mine a couple of times because I am not only lazy but also anxious for the earthworms and other insects to occupy it. They are discouraged by too much heat and will only lurk around the edges.

You can make compost faster by turning it more often but my experience is that plenty of earthworms will make small quantities of wonderful compost in 42 days. Using the plastic backs of old television sets, I make up special mixtures for pot plants and container gardens and I always leave some of the worms and egg capsules in the mixture. If your heap is smelly and anaerobic it will need turning more often, until it smells like newly turned earth rather than something that makes you gag.

COMPOST TINKERERS

If a wide variety of organic material is used it should provide enough of the necessary minerals, but if you are a born tinkerer or a compost-making addict there are a few minerals which you can think about adding.

I always add lime to the heap after every few layers because I want to be sure that the pH is not too acid, or alkaline for that matter, for earthworms. But the other important benefit of adding lime or dolomite is that calcium, an important trace mineral, is added. Calcium is essential for earthworms and their calciferous glands.

I add most of my wood ash to the heap, especially that remaining after burning the woody garden rubbish I am not composting. Wood ash is a great source of potassium but do not add coal ash as it is toxic to plants. While adding charcoal is not recommended because it doesn't break down, I don't mind a little as I believe it helps keep the heap sweet.

Phosphorus, along with the elements nitrogen and potassium (NPK), is essential for plant growth. You can add a little pure rock phosphate if you want, or some superphosphate fertiliser which also contains sulphur, a secondary but important nutrient.

A LITTLE ABOUT NPK

While the NPK of good compost is quite low, its greatest value lies in its slow release of nutrients over a longer period of time. The nutrients in many chemical fertilisers are released faster, although sometimes, unless other essential elements are present in the soil, the nutrient value may remain inert. While fast, high-heat compost is a great fertiliser and should be weed free, the presence of earthworms in cool compost adds valuable castings which enable more of the nutrients and elements to be made available to plants.

When you see the letters and percentages NPK: 10–6–4 on commercial fertilisers, for example, it describes the N for nitrogen (10%), P for phosphorus (6%), and K for potassium (4%) content of the product. N, P and K are the major nutrients essential for healthy plant life and growth.

The minor or secondary nutrients essential for healthy plant life include calcium (Ca), magnesium (Mg) and iron (Fe). Plants also need very tiny quantities of trace elements, including zinc, boron, cobalt, molybdenum, sulphur, copper, chlorine, and manganese.

Nitrogen (N) is important because it is the basis of protein and makes up the body food. Nitrogen is essential for leaf and stem growth and gives plants their healthy green colour.

Phosphorus (P) stimulates growth, flowering and root development in plants. Cell division is impossible without phosphorus and plants that lack this nutrient grow slowly and have a tendency to weak root systems. New Zealand soils have been notoriously deficient in phosphorus.

Potassium (K) is essential to develop chlorophyll and strengthen plant tissue, and makes plants more disease resistant.

A LITTLE ABOUT pH

The pH describes the alkalinity (sweetness) or acidity (sourness) of soil and compost and is usually expressed as a number on a scale of 1 to 14. 1 indicates pure acidity, 4–5 acid, through neutral at 7, 8–9 alkaline to 14 pure alkalinity. Most plants grow best within the neutral zone while most bacteria, fungi and earthworms function best with a pH of 6.6 to about 7.2.

To lessen acidity add lime (calcium carbonate) and to increase acidity add shredded newspaper or peat moss.

Earthworms in the Garden

I must have been temporarily deranged when I bought my present house. I've always fancied myself as a bit of a gardener and landscaper and one of the attractions of the neglected 55-year-old house/city-quarter-acre was the underdeveloped garden. Let's face it, non-existent garden, although privet, honeysuckle and flax jostled for supremacy.

The surrounding hedges were a nightmare of riotous growth and the back of the section was a three-metre burial ground of old car parts, beer cans, weeds, honeysuckle, corrugated iron, spouting, beer cans, weeds, honeysuckle, plastic, ceramic tiles, beer cans, weeds, honeysuckle, household rubbish, beer cans, weeds, honeysuckle, broken glass, kikuyu, grass clippings and beer cans — a real tip. Two former rose gardens had been tastelessly filled in with black plastic and bricks, and previously cultivated areas, including remnants of lawn, contained every weed known to gardeners. Dock, dandelion and thistle abounded. Comfrey thrived. What a challenge!

The good features were two neglected fish ponds, three pongas, a huge grapefruit tree, an old palm and one gnarled but beautiful magnolia. Birds nested everywhere and there were heaps of ladybirds and mantises.

What had I done? The contract rubbish removal, hedge cutting, tree pruning and tip fees confirmed my temporary insanity. However, two-thirds of the way down the burial ground, the remaining suburban jetsam was surrounded by ten or so metres of

Topsoil and burrows

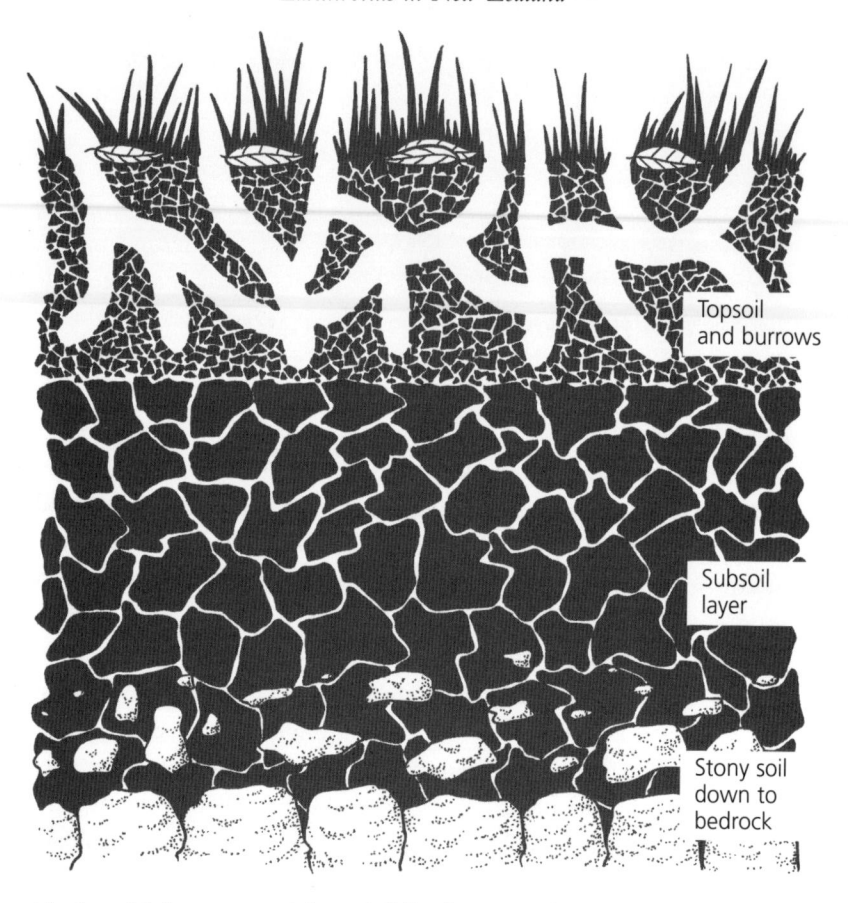

Subsoil layer

Stony soil down to bedrock

black gold, humus so rich and full of worms that I was prepared to pick out the rest of the beer cans, broken glass, metal, foam chips and bits of plastic as I barrowed out the precious humus.

By the time I had planted my precious cuttings, 23 trees, and removed the bricks and polythene, I found that almost the entire section was home to huge populations of earthworms. *L. terrestris, L. rubellus, A. caliginosa* and *A. trapezoides* thrived in the soil, and *E. foetida* resided in my new compost heap and the worm bin I'd brought with me from the north.

I am not suggesting that the way to encourage earthworms is to let your backyard become a festering rubbish tip. I am convinced, however, that seven years of non-cultivation allowed the continual

— Earthworms in the garden —

accumulation of weeds, grass and leaves to provide the earthworms with such a quantity of mineral-rich organic waste that the mixed population exploded. The result? Everything grows here!

I'm learning and will continue to learn valuable lessons as I develop this garden. The first and possibly most important is the same concept that applies to making compost; you letting nature help you, and not overdeveloping your garden to such a stage that there is no room for a weed or two. Some casual disorder might be a good idea, even, dare I say it, a dandelion-, dock- and comfrey-infested corner.

A few other lessons. If I ever wondered whether deep digging was necessary I'm now convinced. It's not. If I ever doubted the value of no-dig or raised gardens, mineral-rich weeds, mulches, and not cultivating around citrus trees, I doubt no more. The earthworms have clearly demonstrated many things I'd previously read about but not practised.

There's a downside for some. If you're the sort of person who throws the kitchen waste down the sink, an extremely tidy person who hates seeing a few leaves lying about, tweaks out weeds at their first appearance, likes to clip and burn errant vines or throw out piles of grass, can't bear the wormcasts which appear every autumn in a worm-friendly garden, likes unmulched bare soil in the vegetable garden and sprays for every pest imaginable, then encouraging earthworms to live in your garden is not a good idea.

The other downside is that where you have a full house or garden of worms, the lawn won't look too good for a couple of months in the autumn and, especially around citrus trees, the ground will be spongy because of the amount of casting activity. I suppose you could throw a mulch of hay about. It won't look very tidy, but think about that underground city of worms. My gumboots and I are prepared to live with it. Besides, the fruit is healthy and delicious.

PRACTICES TO ENCOURAGE EARTHWORKERS

How you encourage the spread of earthworms in your garden depends on the size of your section. As I've already talked about my quarter-acre section let's continue to look at the slightly larger garden. We're mainly talking earthworkers — the soil-dwellers — here, although the composters do their share.

• Think about a mixed earthworm community (see page 37) and remember that the key to increasing populations as well as improving the soil's fertility and structure is to regularly add extra organic material, compost or mulches to the soil. Put simply, if you want more, add more. If you think the population is high enough you will still need to keep adding compost and mulches to maintain the population and keep up the soil fertility, but only at a maintenance level.

• Keep up the composting of every bit of waste organic material you can get your hands on. Your local greengrocer, supermarket and so on may be good sources. Check out neighbours who put grass clippings in the 'green bin' for the tip. Encourage people who pay to take green waste to be composted to drop it at your place for free. Take the children to the park to collect bags of leaves and make a special leaf mould bin. Have one or two comfrey plants and regularly add the leaves to the compost heap. Take a Sunday drive and collect or buy horse or chicken manure. Visit the seashore after a storm to collect seaweed. Wander through the pine forest and collect a small bag of pine needles. During the months of May to July you might also find delicious lemon-coloured cepes as well. If in doubt check them out.

• If you're planning a bark garden in a damp weedy area, don't spray with weedkiller first. Instead, mow the weeds closely then thoroughly wet the area. Mulch with a 10-mm layer of wet newspaper and soaked cardboard, overlapping around trees and shrubs. Wet the area thoroughly. Spread the bark mulch and forget about weeds coming through. The close mowing will have knocked back the tops, lack of sunshine will inhibit further growth, and earthworms will get to work on the roots and decomposing weeds. Activity under the newspaper will be high. Follow this procedure as well when you're putting in raised or no-dig gardens, but in this case add plenty of compost worms to the organic material *on top of*

the newspaper. Composting is fun and saves you money.
• There are rare occasions when it is necessary to use a weedkiller, in driveways, around buildings and fencelines. I have used the herbicide Roundup to good effect and as it is absorbed through the foliage and moves down through the plant, not the soil, it does not affect the earthworm population. Living up north I found that when I reluctantly started using it on a limestone and gravel driveway, within a month or so of damp weather, earthworms (*A. caliginosa* and *L. rubellus*) congregated in high numbers where I had sprayed, devouring the remnant root systems. (From conversations with soil scientists I can say that most herbicides have few negative effects on earthworms and where they increase the amount of organic material in the soil they can be considered beneficial. The same cannot be said for pesticides, which are generally detrimental, and fungicides, which are often toxic.)
• If you have lots of dandelion, dock and other weeds in the lawn, as I have, you can use Roundup or try my slower and more tedious method which, I warn you, will take probably two or three years to get a perfect lawn. Cut the weeds out at ground level before they seed, leaving the roots behind for underground activity. After the grass growth and earthworm casting has slowed (say June) drag a metal rake through the lawn in every direction to aerate the soil and spread the castings. Fill in any hollows with a commercial shrub and tree mixture. Topdress all over with a fine layer of the shrub and tree mixture, having added more worm castings from your backyard earthworm bin, or a small bag from an earthworm grower. Use compost instead of the sterilised commercial mix providing it is weed free. If you decide to use Roundup, aerate the soil once the weeds have wilted and then follow the other steps.
• Mix castings from your worm bin with any commercial potting, tub or patio, tree or shrub preparation you use to give new plantings a boost and get them established quickly. Add egg capsules and tiny earthworms from your bin directly into the soil around new trees, shrubs, roses and other precious plants. Topdress vegetables and seedlings with castings and mix just below the

surface. Liquid worm manure or castings will give all plants a great boost and any new trees having problems will benefit.
• Every home garden should have a breeding worm box or bin as well as a compost pile, to make the castings and egg capsules you will need.

Smaller sites

Shrinking section sizes and inner city apartments do not mean that earthworms cannot work for you. With a small section space is important, and if you compost your efforts will be confined to a small commercial bin. You may have decks and paved areas,

---

LEAF MOULD AND GREEN GRASS SILAGE

Leaves take longer to break down in the compost heap so keeping a container or bin specifically for making leaf mould, the very best humus, might be a good idea. The fungi that work their way through leaves are different from those in the compost heap, but earthworms will approve of any special arrangements you make for their benefit.

After a heavy fall of rain gather the leaves into a small enclosed heap or bin, or stuff them into black plastic rubbish bags where you can ignore them. Add a sprinkling of lime and blood and bone and a couple of spadefuls of worm-filled compost to encourage faster activity. Make sure everything is really moist before closing the bag or covering the heap.

It will be many months before the leaves have partially rotted and the heap consolidated. They can be used then as a wonderful mulch, dug into the soil to improve structure, or else be left for another few months and then used instead of peat in potting mix. I use the partially rotted leaves in one of my special worm compost mixtures.

If you have access to piles of grass clippings use the same method to make green grass silage, but be sure to allow the grass to heat and cool before you pile the clippings into bags, otherwise the worms will die from the heat and you will have a stinking mess. Use more lime with grass than with leaves.

---

meaning that contact with the soil is confined to large pots and containers, and hanging baskets to utilise the air space.

In city apartments or flats, potential gardening space is even more important. Herbs on a kitchen window, houseplants, container gardening, hanging baskets, and if you're lucky a small balcony, will have to satisfy your urge to garden. Space restrictions will not allow you to store bags of fertiliser, potting mix and so on.

If a small earthworm farm is necessary for larger city sections, it is even more important for people with smaller sections and in flats or apartments. Here we're talking only composting worms, that is *E. foetida* and *L. rubellus*. They will dispose of kitchen and container gardening waste and provide you with as many castings as you will need to fertilise your gardening efforts. You can keep the farm in the garden shed, the laundry or on the balcony.

On a small section your earthworm farm can be as small or as large as space will allow. You could use an old laundry tub, washing machine bowl or a large plastic barrel cut in half lengthwise. Whatever you use the container will need drainage and air holes, and if you use a metal or treated timber container, seal the surface with paraffin wax. Be inventive.

I started using the plastic covers from the backs of television sets to make small earthworm farms to take to displays. The air vents were a bonus for getting extra oxygen into the worm bed and made the container perfect. Easy to carry around, not unsightly to look at, home to about 4,000 worms and plenty of egg capsules when in full production. I use a different mix if I'm making special compost but for the ordinary purpose I use half-rotted compost, rotting hay, grass clippings and horse manure mixed with hay or sawdust. It makes a perfect medium for earthworms to live in, providing food and warmth. After a fortnight to three weeks I feed them once a week on horse manure and occasionally kitchen waste. You can tell when the worms need further food because the bed surface is flat and covered with fine castings.

Don't believe anyone who tells you that composting worms will live on a mixture of soil and the odd lettuce leaf. That might do

A. caliginosa for a couple of days, but *E. foetida* needs lush organic material to survive.

You can use either this mixture or a combination of half-rotted compost, shredded paper, horse manure or commercial sheep pellets, lawn clippings and decomposing leaves. Feed on kitchen waste, whatever organic waste you have (vacuum cleaner dust) or a poultry mix. Do not put meat scraps or bones into the bed, as this may encourage flies. A deep tray under the bin or bed will catch any liquid run-off which, diluted with water, makes an excellent potplant fertiliser.

A decent-sized rubbish tin, or other suitable plastic container with drainage holes in the bottom and a few air holes in the sides, will make a good bed, and there are other containers in other materials which might be pressed into service. Handy people are making suitable containers. Don't forget the drip catcher.

In a small apartment the television container or a smaller rubbish tin would be ideal, or you could invest in the Reln Can O'Worms being sold throughout the country.

If you are only using your worm farm to dispose of kitchen waste you will not need much bedding because the earthworms will quickly make their own medium to live in. In this case put 5 cm of soil in the container and add 1,000–1,500 worms. Add the food on top of the soil, sprinkle with a little lime and top up twice a week. Kitchen waste produces lots of castings and liquid manure so make sure your under-bin container is big enough to cope. Excess liquid fertiliser can be stored for a few months. A word of warning: an excess of fruit pulp or waste will encourage fruit flies so keep a cover on.

The smaller the worm fodder the faster the worms will deal to it. For example, chop a banana skin into four or five pieces. I keep a covered container on my sinkbench and chop things as I put them in. Children's leftover rice, cereal, vegetables etc. make excellent food. Once the container is full of vermicast, a mixture of worms, egg capsules and castings, start the process over again. Give away your excess worms.

— *Earthworms in the garden* —

Use the castings mixed, say 40:60, with potting mix for new plants or to repot old ones. Give existing plants a surface feed with pure castings. Flush your orchid plants with water in the usual way and then fertilise with the diluted liquid manure. My collection of dendrobiums thrive on this. The castings/potting mix medium is great for growing small containers of lush fancy lettuce, herbs and other salad greens on the balcony. Don't overlook tall containers with side pockets that go up as well as ones that spread out.

If you'd like to grow extra-lush begonias and gloxinias use a large tall pot, put a quarter of your castings/potting mix medium in the bottom, add a layer of commercial sheep pellets, put in another quarter of mix, and add some egg capsules and small worms from the bin. Fill the container, water it thoroughly and plant. Once the plant is established, water one time in four with liquid worm fertiliser. Adding a couple of handfuls of Aquasoil to the mix will help retain moisture. Return the worms to the bed or give them away at the end of the growing season.

Earthworms in Pasture

The 1982 Invermay Research Station Report

Since 1945 New Zealand soil scientists have been studying earthworms and their effects on pasture. Without exception their wide-ranging studies continue to show that plant growth can be increased and the soil structure in pasture improved by using the *Lumbricidae* earthworms, originally introduced accidentally from Europe.

In 1982 Dr J.A. Springett, Mr G.G. Cossens, Dr P. Pottinger and Dr T.E.T. Trought from the Ministry of Agriculture & Fisheries Research Division and Mr R. Kent and Mr M.J. Stockdill from the the Advisory Services Division, all with a common interest in earthworms, met at the Invermay Research Station to review the research and see how the productivity of New Zealand farms might be increased using beneficial earthworms.

The most important of the recommendations to come out of this meeting were: to carry out a national survey on the earthworm status of New Zealand soils; to further research earthworm introduction, ecology and benefits to crops; and to introduce earthworms to the New Zealand soils which lacked the appropriate species.

Now, a leaner, hungrier, market-driven New Zealand might be what is needed for soil scientists to put their plans into action. They will still need funding, either by government agencies or by private sponsorship, but it is to be hoped that the money men will recognise the long-term benefits of investing in a plan to spread beneficial earthworms into New Zealand pastures.

So, apart from a strong interest and belief in the value of beneficial earthworms, what was the main reason for the 1982 recommendations?

I'm only guessing, but perhaps the most compelling reason (and the one most likely to influence the money providers) can be found in the summary of Dr Jo Springett's 1982 report of that meeting. I quote:

'Large areas of New Zealand lack an adequate earthworm population, either topsoil mixing or deep burrowing species. It is estimated that earthworm introduction could increase the carrying capacity of at least 4.5 million hectares of pasture by between one and 2.5 stock units per hectare over the next two decades. This represents a potential increase in annual export earnings of between $200 million and $500 million p.a. for an initial single investment of about $10 per hectare ($45 million).'

Remember that this was written in 1982 so the cost benefit, even with a higher initial investment, would have to be considerably more. Land is still an indivisible resource. Remember too that these were not figures out of the air being bandied about by the committee. They were farm advisory officer and researcher M.J. Stockdill's figures for a cost benefit analysis previously published in Aglink FPP 211 in 1981.

In discussing the Southland/Otago and the Volcanic Plateau regions, both areas lacking topsoil mixing species, Dr Springett wrote that an increased pasture production of between 10 and 20

If the 1982 recommendations had been fully implemented the face of New Zealand agriculture would have changed markedly, but unfortunately the cataclysmic changes which shook New Zealand from 1984 onward not only delayed their plans, but also slowed down other important earthworm research. The necessary funds were not and still are not readily available.

percent could be expected after the introduction of a topsoil mixing species like *A. caliginosa* or *A. rosea*, and at least one extra stock unit per hectare could be supported. The time taken to increase the pasture production would be about seven years, so no instant returns from introducing earthworms to pasture would be evident.

Returning to Mr Ashmore's previously mentioned 864-acre Raetihi property, it took over 15 years of systematic earthworm planting of the paddocks to cover 700 acres. In an official trial started in 1941 along a hill slope, single sods were placed in a line about one chain apart for several chains. By 1944 the earthworms had worked up and down the slope some $1^1/_2$ to 2 chains from the original line of planting. The optimistic estimate in 1945 was that it would take four to five years for a single planting of earthworms to cover and populate an acre of land.

Of course, the more plantings made the less time it would take, but as Dr Springett points out, the time lag before the pasture production increased might lessen farmers' motivation and enthusiasm for planting earthworms. In seven years the farm could have changed hands and other management changes like topdressing, giving rapid and visible results, might have already increased pasture production. So while the benefits of planting earthworms are pretty well guaranteed, farmers need to realise that pasture improvement takes time.

Every farm is different and every farmer has become more economically driven. As never before, farming is a business and each farmer will have a differing viewpoint about priorities; how they might get the best out of their land and stock, improve their investment and earn a decent living. A classic example of this is given in the report:

'The committee visited farms which had had earthworms introduced to some paddocks over the past 20 years and while the farmers were certain that the wormed paddocks were the most productive, they had not felt any need to spread worms to the rest of their farms.'

Fifteen years on, harsher economic realities might find those

— *Earthworms in pasture* —

same farmers reacting differently and spreading earthworms as fast as they can go. So what can they do?

How earthworms benefit pasture

There are three reasons why large areas of New Zealand still contain no beneficial earthworms. One is that the beneficial species were accidentally introduced to New Zealand, mainly as egg capsules in the roots of English trees or in the soil ballast of early ships. So the original spread of earthworms was often dependent on where the settlers planted those trees and where the ballast soil was dumped.

The second reason is that there are large areas where the soil conditions — pH and so on — make the environment unfriendly, and until that is corrected earthworms will not thrive.

The third is that sometimes beneficial species are not found simply because they have never been introduced to the area.

Where populations have been established the physical and biological properties of soil have been altered to the extent that pasture production increases of more than 70 percent have been recorded, so it is clearly worthwhile encouraging earthworms to settle at your place.

With plenty of beneficial earthworms in pasture the soil structure is improved and nutrients are made more readily available. Topsoil and surface grazing species like *L. rubellus* and *A. caliginosa* eat the surface litter and dung, preventing a turf mat layer and allowing better lime, fertiliser and water penetration and an easier vertical distribution of grassgrub-controlling insecticide.

A. caliginosa, which gets most of its food underground, also breaks

---

A pasture can carry as great or an even greater weight of earthworms beneath it as the livestock above it, so equal care and attention should be given to the needs of stock living under the soil surface, as to the needs of stock living above the surface.

---

down the root mat build-up and can convert it to humus within three years. Apart from improving the soil's moisture-holding capacity and water infiltration rate, the root mat reduction allows more rapid heat exchange and extends the growing season by making the pasture warmer by night and cooler by day.

The result is more rapid grass or plant germination, faster growth and healthier, more stress-resistant plants, another good reason for stimulating and encouraging large populations.

Lower dwelling species like *A. longa* directly affect the soil structure by eating their way through it and making it more friable. Opening up the compact soils again improves water infiltration and retention which reduces run-off, erosion and flooding. The improved friability lessens the risk of wind erosion.

If there are no earthworms in your soil you must first establish why they are not there. If it is simply because they have never been introduced in the region the problem is possibly easy to solve. But if conditions exist which keep the earthworms out (see page 20), planting them without addressing these conditions is pointless.

Earthworm activity can often be kept at a desirable level by using the correct soil management practices rather than introducing earthworms artificially. You may only need to modify previous soil management methods, like the calcium levels, to allow the worms to establish themselves to an effective density. So the first steps to either establishing or improving the beneficial species are to do an earthworm population count and then soil tests.

COUNTING EARTHWORM POPULATIONS

The best time of the year to count earthworm populations is in the late autumn or early spring when the ground is soft and the earthworm activity high. Choose a paddock with good grass cover and dig out selected squares of turf about 25 cm across and 20 cm deep, say 4 metres apart, throughout or diagonally across the paddock.

Count every earthworm in each square, and include egg capsules if any are present. The population can be considered significant if your samples each contain at least ten earthworms. If there are only one or two in each sample, that will tell you that earthworms are contributing very little to the physical condition of the soil.

If your pasture contains any extras like dandelion, chicory or thistle, make sure that several samples include these plants to see whether there is a greater congregation around the thicker and deeper penetrating roots, especially during the drier summer season.

An easier, but less accurate, way to count populations and species in a given area is to connect an electric fence unit to water pipes laid a few metres apart on the dampened area and run an electric current through it. The small worms will appear quickly, followed shortly after by the larger worms and the deeper burrowing species. This method will give you an idea of the population rather than a precise count.

I didn't like giving the earthworms a charge when I tried this, but if you want to collect earthworms by this method, either to count, sell, store or to seed pasture, choose a cloudy and damp day, and preferably late afternoon. The worms must be kept cool. If you are seeding pasture, separate the species if possible, and hold the worms, at least overnight, in boxes of roughly one-third well watered soil or castings, one-third humus or decaying leaf matter, and one-third finely crushed animal manure. If your pasture seeding is held up, the earthworms should remain quite happily in the boxes until needed.

Other means of counting populations involve taking core samples and using irritant chemicals like formalin to extract the worms (see Bibliography).

CREATING AN EARTHWORM-FRIENDLY ENVIRONMENT

So you've got the results of your soil tests, counted the earthworms, and discovered beneficial species present but in very low numbers. How do you create an environment in which earthworms will multiply and thrive?

Soil tests and fertilisers

Be guided by the results of your soil tests and correct any deficiencies in sulphur, calcium, phosphate or other minerals, and apply the recommended organic dusts and fertilisers — dolomite, feldspar, sulphur, magnesium, langbinite.

Organic rock phosphate fertiliser gives excellent results and can be used in place of superphosphate, although Dr Springett told me that in 15 years of earthworm study she had found no evidence that phosphates harmed earthworms, unless excessive use caused a very low pH. Phosphates usually increase earthworm populations and soil fertility.

The beneficial effects of superphosphate are confirmed by Lincoln University Professor T.W. Walker's research. He says that superphosphate stimulates clover growth and biological nitrogen fixation, and once eaten is excreted mainly as urea in urine, stimulating grass growth. The extra growth increases the stock carrying capacity and therefore leads to more dung, building up the organic matter in the soil and stimulating earthworm numbers to increase.

Perhaps a lingering 'bad press' for phosphates comes from confusion over the European use of nitrate fertilisers, some of which, sulphate of ammonia and nitrate of soda, can be harmful to earthworms.

Earthworms need lime, and it should be applied whenever earthworms are being introduced or in correcting unfriendly situations. Once the earthworm populations have been established a maintenance level of liming will need sustaining to avoid leaching caused by increased water infiltration.

Aerate the soil and avoid compressing and trampling
One of the fastest ways to improve soil is to aerate it, the major proviso being opening, not turning or ploughing the soil. Once the corrective nutrients have been applied even shallow ploughing can interrupt the earthworms' attempts to establish themselves. And in established populations one deep ploughing can reduce the colonies by up to 40 percent. Where earthworms have been introduced or are being encouraged to spread, if at all possible pasture should not be ploughed or cultivated for seven years after their introduction.

So where you must open the soil, use a deep chisel plough ripper which will open the surface cover, or harrows which will open and aerate a greater surface area and help spread any surface dung into the soil. Once the topsoil dwellers have become established there will be no further need for you to do this as the earthworms will pull the dung down themselves and their very presence will mean greater soil aeration. There is no doubt that earthworm populations, especially the deep burrowing species, increase when crops are planted by direct drilling in undisturbed soils.

Avoid any activity which will compress the soil and reduce that aerating process. The pasture will grow better, water will drain faster, earthworms can move through the soil more easily and essential micro-organisms will multiply faster when the soil is kept friable. Even walking over the soil in your backyard garden will compact it, so in pasture avoid overgrazing or driving tractors and so on all over the paddocks, and where cropping is planned, get it in as soon as possible.

Where the winter sees a decrease in earthworm numbers on cultivated land it may be due to insufficient organic debris or lack of a protective cover. The winter is when earthworms' physical activity is at a peak, and to thrive they need plenty of food. If there isn't enough food or cover they may leave the paddock in search of more hospitable areas, but they are more likely to die.

The living environment can often be improved a great deal in just a single winter by providing a cover which will protect both the existing and the expanding colony. Giving them a cover crop or an insulating layer of mulch, hay or manure will keep the nutrients and moisture in the root zone near the surface and help them survive, and as the cover breaks down it will provide extra food. Again, once the population has been established the earthworms will work the soil, granulating and making it porous and increasing the fertility for the following season.

Stock fodder

While some fortunate farmers have grazing units which enable them to rotate their stock and use deferred grass for feeding, many others still rely on supplements like hay, silage, or crops. I cannot emphasise too strongly, in every instance where grass has been cut for silage or for hay, or crops cut for feeding out, that retaining the remaining stubble or growth provides food for *A. caliginosa* and *L. rubellus* to process and mix with soil. It also provides insulation and helps to moderate soil temperatures. Even when allowing stock to graze on the remainder of the crop it pays to leave remnants behind for earthworms. On no account fire up the remaining stubble.

Water conservation
It is worth repeating that without water earthworms cannot survive because they are unable to conserve moisture. Moisture does not mean waterlogged, however, so until the water infiltration and porosity rate has been improved by numerous burrows and more friable soil, excess water will need draining.

Your land may be in one of those unfortunate 'dry in summer, wet in winter' zones where it is necessary to channel around and through the pasture, to take away surplus water in winter and to use for irrigation during summer.

Where *A. longa* has been established in soils likely to crack on drying out, the water infiltration rates decrease in summer and increase in winter. Improving the soil texture means fewer cracks opening in the surface of the wormed areas and once the autumn rains arrive the surface soil absorbs water faster. It appears that in irrigated soils the water acceptance rate may be more closely related to the number of earthworms present than to any other soil factor, and when soil moisture is improved earthworms will increase their populations.

Occasionally large quantities of earthworms may be collected after hay is cut and before it is turned. Frequently earthworms, especially *A. caliginosa* and *L. rubellus*, will spend the night after cutting on the surface under the hay.

The right pasture

When sowing new or replacing pasture grass the right grass is very important. Choosing perennial pasture for traditionally dry land will provide cover to help lower the soil temperature in summer, and food from the plant debris and dead roots. Planting a selection of deep rooting pastures will give stock above and below the ground a choice of grass and roughage. This selection could include herbs like chicory, yarrow and dandelion, and winter feed supplements like willow which can be grazed or cut as required. Even in the driest summer earthworms not taking a dive will congregate around chicory and dandelion roots.

Trees and shelter belts

In 1992 when outrageous prices were offered for *Pinus radiata* and other species, many Northland farmers (and no doubt others throughout the country) were seduced into cutting down their shelter belts. While there were occasions when the cutting could possibly be justified, I found it hard to believe that these temporary owners of the land could be so stupid. Market driven indeed!

Trees provide so much to a beneficial farming environment and if you have ever seen parched and heat-stressed cattle and sheep looking for shelter or huddled under a lone pine in the Northland

Farmers who provide a sympathetic living environment for beneficial earthworms should see populations established and spreading rapidly (for earthworms) within two or three years, although it will take around seven years before a high density of six million or more per hectare can be expected. Earthworm saturation in the soil environment is not a speedy process. However, once the biomass has been established farmers can expect excellent yields in pasture and crops, higher stocking capability, and other benefits like lower water run-off, less soil erosion, and huge savings in fertiliser bills. A rhythmic cycle will have been set up and providing there is no break in the cycle there should be no break in the higher production figures and benefits.

heat you will understand what I mean. But besides the shelter they provide, they also help retain soil moisture and provide wind breaks to reduce the moisture loss from pasture. As far as the stock below the ground are concerned, there is seldom a shelter belt or stand of trees which does not have healthy earthworm populations living under and around it.

Where a forestry project, possibly tree crops, is included in a farm business, far from taking pasture away from stock, it can increase returns by eventually providing grazing for cattle and leaf drop for earthworms, building more humus for healthy soil, and a long term increase in the crop yield. Dung from the grazing stock provides more earthworm food to be incorporated into the soil.

The need for trees is obvious and their inclusion in farm management strategy should be automatic.

INTRODUCING EARTHWORMS TO NEW AREAS

Assuming that soil tests have been carried out and any corrective measures taken, it is probably easier to establish new colonies of beneficial species, especially in moist soils which favour the establishment, spread and activity of earthworms, than to correct mistakes in land management.

New Zealand farm advisory officer Murray Stockdill has developed a simple method of introducing earthworms to pasture (described in Aglink FPP 211). For the benefit of farmers unable to get this paper I quote from the 1982 Invermay Report.

'An area rich in the required earthworm species (usually *A. caliginosa* and *L. rubellus*) is identified and turf cut into 20-cm squares to a depth of 8 cm. These turfs are then placed, sward side down, on the pasture to be inoculated. If the pH of the pasture is less than 5.6 and the quick test calcium less than 5 then a dressing of lime at a rate of 2 tonnes per ha is applied only in the immediate vicinity of the worm turf at the time of inoculation.

'A dressing of lime at that rate may be recommended for the whole paddock in year five or six. When the turfs are placed on a 20-m grid pattern, the worms from the turfs will colonise the pasture and will start to make a significant improvement in production at about the 5th to 9th year after inoculation. In pastures with a heavy turf mat the initial increase in production may be more than twice the eventual steady state increase.'

Mr Stockdill has also developed a turf cutting machine which works best on close grazed pasture and gently rolling country. It can be attached to a tractor along with a spreading machine which sows a square metre of lime every 10 metres and places a turf, grass-side down, on each limed square. Placing them grass-side down prevents the turfs from taking root, and provides good contact with the ground and a food supply of semi-rotting pasture for the migrating worms. There is an Ag Report video available that shows this machine in operation and it certainly makes the procedure look easy. Plans for both machines are available and an engineering shop should be able to make one for you.

The work must be done under moist conditions when the maximum number of worms (say 20–40) is in the top 50–75 mm of the source area. A hectare of high producing source material should provide sufficient turf to seed 1,000 hectares of land, so huge areas of source material are not needed.

Even where large areas of pasture are not populated, a suitable area should be found on most properties, except where lumbricids have never been introduced. Look for them close to old homestead sites or near old established shelter belts, especially those of deciduous trees.

The source areas are easier to find when the soils are wet and the worms are casting freely on the surface. Areas that are obviously greener than their surroundings in early spring are the most likely.

Land conformation and finance might make it easier for some to take turf in the old fashioned way, with a plough and a spade, and spread it manually from the back of the tractor. There are a few drawbacks which may have stopped farmers using this method in the past. The work needs two people to cut and spread the turf, in the right weather conditions, so time and planning is necessary. Another is that time lag, especially when farmers like to see rapid results. They need to know that they're still going to be farming the same property for a long time.

The third drawback lies with farmers having insufficient information and therefore becoming confused over what method to use. They need sound advice on the nearest source of useful worms and the most efficient way to introduce the worms onto their farms. Finally, having to move large, heavy quantities of soil with the worms (up to 5 tonnes per hectare) limits the turf sowing method to areas with reasonable access, or else increases the costs of getting the turf to the site.

If you can grow your own, get access to or are able to buy beneficial species it will make the job a little easier. I have only paddled around the edges of this, but experiments by qualified people indicate that it is possible to breed *A. caliginosa* and *A. longa* in reasonable quantities in an organic material/soil mix. But, according to Dr Springett, the method is prone to inexplicable failures. It is worth persevering, however, because the worms produced are large specimens, ideal for introduction and only half the amount of soil is needed to transport them.

Should you find a breeder with stock to sell, be prepared to pay around $80 a thousand, maybe more, a not unreasonable figure considering the difficulties involved in breeding or collecting, or when you consider that planting 20 at a time gives you 50 breeding sites. John Stemmer from Motueka, the pioneer of farmed earthworms in New Zealand, might just know more about collecting and breeding *A. caliginosa* than anyone else around, and in the autumn and winter is busy filling as many orders as he can supply with pasture worms.

So you might have to try breeding them yourself. I have already mentioned collecting species in wet weather and keeping them in containers to plant or breed from (see page 71).

Box breeding of *Aporrectodea caliginosa*

If you are going to try this do not expect these worms to breed in the same densities as *E. foetida*. Drill several pencil-sized holes in the bottom and sides of a large bin, basin or box and line the box with damp rotting hay. Collect the worms, count them and place them in the bed with equal parts of damp soil, finely crushed manure (not chicken) and wilted fine grass or decomposing leaves. Place another layer of hay on top, and cover with carpet and polythene. Keep the bed damp at all times. Put something hard on top, concrete or cinder block.

These are the only beds which I keep in ground contact. The ground holes are not there for drainage but to allow the worms to escape if they don't like the conditions, so be sure you know the number of worms placed in the bed. So far my two basins are thriving as to size, and there are some capsules and a few small worms. Surprisingly few are choosing to escape.

My collection for this bed came from under the bricks on my defunct rose gardens. Large numbers of *L. rubellus* and *A. caliginosa* had made a temporary home between the bricks and heavy duty polythene. I have no idea why they chose to live here.

The following autumn, introduce them to a particular area, making sure the soil is damp and that you have limed extensively first, say 200 g for each chosen spot. Cut out the top layer of grass and root growth to a depth of about 50 mm. Put in a thin layer of finely crushed manure mixed with a little fine soil. Dampen. Add ten worms and replace the turf grass-side down.

Breeding *Aporrectodea longa*

A. longa is now considered to be a beneficial lower-dwelling species to plant and cultivate, although it will be many years before the long-term benefits of adding this species to the soil mix can be calculated. But if you have access to any *A. longa*, you can try Dr Springett's method of breeding them in natural 'farmed' conditions. She said (in 1984) that *A. longa* would have to be sold for 50 cents to $1 each to make it commercially viable.

Collect 200 *A. longa* if you can, although you may have to make do with less. Make an alternate layered heap of soil and sheep manure, each layer 100–150 mm deep, and sprinkled with 200 g/m^2 (1 kg/5m^2) of lime. The entire heap should be 0.75–1 m deep and surrounded by baled straw or hay. Seed the layers with

Utilising space and shade

50 mature *A. longa* per m² in late winter. Keep it moist by watering monthly until water runs out the bottom, and add further lime in mid-summer to maintain the pH at the right level. (If sheep have been regularly drenched with an anthelmintic like Ivermectin the manure may not be a good food source.)

The following winter, cart the compost out to the paddocks and drop a spadeful at a time at grid spacings of about 10 m by 10 m which have been limed at 200 g/m². Each spadeful of compost should include three to five mature worms plus some young and egg capsules.

A 2 m² x 1 m deep heap of compost should provide enough worms to introduce to around 8 hectares of pasture and to seed another breeding bin for the following year.

Breeding *Eisenia foetida* on the farm

It would seem foolish not to utilise any excess organic waste or manure on a pig, horse or dairy farm, and a large scale composting site can be set up without too much trouble. Check the copper levels in pig manure. Too high a content can be toxic to worms.

Follow the general instructions for making compost (see page 51) but add copious amounts of last season's hay to the layers of manure and lime and make sure that the heaps are continually damp. Very little heat should be generated and *E. foetida* can be introduced immediately; within a very short space of time they will be multiplying at a tremendous rate and reducing the waste material to vermicompost, containing castings, small worms and egg capsules.

All of this material, including the worms, can be used on pastures and around trees or incorporated into croplands, either by drying and spraying or broadcasting by hand. Compost worms will not survive for long unless you reproduce on site similar conditions to those of the compost heap. So add lime and more manure when spreading the vermicompost. Once the egg capsules hatch some of them will survive for quite a period of time.

If your vermicompost includes *L. rubellus* they will have a better chance of survival if the capsules have hatched in situ, because *L. rubellus* is a surface feeder. The nutritional value of the vermicast will give a boost to pasture health and the micro-organisms. Finally, the dead bodies of the worms will give a last boost to the microlife of the soil, adding protein and decomposing food.

Putting it into Practice

Wildwood Farm, Matamata. 106 hectares of gently rolling pasture, soil type Mairoa ash. Farming grazing replacement dairy heifers on a weight gain contract.

When Labour became the Government in 1984 one of their early initiatives was to stop subsidising fertiliser. Superphosphate went up overnight some 700 percent, from $36 per tonne to $200 per tonne, with the upshot that for some considerable time — years in some cases — minimal fertiliser was applied to much of the pastureland in New Zealand.

In successful farming fertiliser is one of the most important tools, and it should be one of the last things to go when the belt is being tightened, because grass production drops so quickly.

Arthur and Julie Payze, with their two small children Abby and Tate, took over Wildwood Farm in June 1992. It was the worst winter Matamata had seen for 15 years and it was pretty much of a shocker for the Payze family as well. Because minimal fertiliser had been applied for seven years there was insufficient grass to feed the 280 dairy heifers which they were contract grazing, and when winter finished only 150 of the original stock remained. To add to their problems Arthur and Julie had no money to apply fertiliser, essential to increase the pasture growth and raise the stocking level.

In the autumn of 1993 the Payzes borrowed money to buy an initial 20 tonnes of fertiliser — a burnt lime and reactive rock phosphate mix — which was applied to about 50 hectares of pasture, and six tonnes of MAP. The investment paid off and the stock numbers were not only sustained but increased to 290. In autumn 1994, 27 tonnes of organic super was applied over specific areas; the stock level was increased to 330. In January 1995, 45 tonnes of organic super was applied over the whole farm, and in their fourth year, winter 1995, they were grazing 350 dairy heifers.

Arthur and Julie's decision to change the way the farm had been run and their belief in the necessity of fertiliser has paid off. Now the farm is an all grass system and the returns have gone from $4.50 to $6.00 per head per week. They have target weight for the animals and targets for the year's growth. The growth rates are monitored carefully and by dividing the dry pasture weight by the necessary animal feeds, the feed per head, even for specific animals, can be increased if necessary.

When Arthur and Julie took over the farm in 1992, the Olson P (the measure of fertility; P = phosphate) was eight and falling. By applying phosphate over the next four years, the P level has steadily increased. One particular measurement has seen the application of 26 units of phosphate give a lift in the P level over six months from 16 to 23. Tests for fertility are taken at least each 12 months. The Olson P level on the Payze farm is now 25 and still rising.

Arthur is in no doubt that the increase in fertility and ability to carry stock has been achieved by the utilisation of organic super and the subsequent increase in the numbers of earthworms carried in the soil. It was essential to regain the fertility that had been decreased by insufficient fertiliser since 1985.

He is also in no doubt that by continuing his organic fertiliser regime, now on a maintenance plus basis dictated by the animals' dry matter requirements, he will ultimately be able to increase the pasture's stock carrying capability to around 600 head. His methods also allow for the addition of essential trace elements necessary, for example, for a high conception rate.

Apart from the Payzes' capability for hard work, what qualities are contained in the organic super that they have used and which

has helped improve the farm so quickly, and how does it compare with superphosphate?
 1. It is possible to apply less fertiliser to get the same P lift.
 2. Higher pH than super phosphate.
 3. Higher organic matter content than super phosphate.
 4. Higher calcium content than super phosphate.
 5. Large percentage of available phosphate and sulphur.
 6. Full range of trace elements.
 7. On the ground cost comparable to if not cheaper than superphosphate.
 8. Gives a lift in P levels which would have cost more in superphosphate.

And what of the earthworms? We walked over much of the farm on an early autumn day before any real rainfall had occurred, so the soil was pretty dry. Everywhere we dug and counted earthworms there were at least three or four beneficial species: *A. caliginosa, A. rosea, A. trapezoides* and *L. rubellus*.

What was surprising considering the lack of soil moisture was the number of earthworms present in the upper levels. I would have expected a high proportion of the population to have retreated to the cooler and damper depths. Where there was chicory or thistle growing, there were inevitably more worms clustered around the root structure.

While it all looked pretty good to me Arthur tells me that in the better paddocks he has earthworm populations of 10,000,000 per hectare or higher. He did not introduce any beneficial earthworms to any of this pasture but rather he improved their environment. Clearly it has paid off.

Arthur believes that his increase in production and stock carrying capability is due to the organic fertiliser and the earthworm populations. No doubt this is true, but I don't believe that the real benefits from his increased earthworm numbers have begun to kick in yet. What has been achieved in four years is amazing, but I believe that the Payzes are due for some pleasant surprises on their farm for many years to come.

EARTHWORMS IN ORCHARDS AND FOODCROPS

There are many people who hate to garden and this book is probably not for them. There are people who expect their gardens to produce bounteous crops of vegetables, fruit and flowers without returning sustenance to the soil. This book should be a help to them. Then there are those who prove the saying 'rubbish in, rubbish out' to be a fallacy. This book was written for farmers and gardeners who, working with nature, turn their organic waste into the very life-blood of the soil, humus. These are the people who take care of the microlife and macro-inhabitants of the soil by returning to the earth that which comes from the earth.

As the earth's populations continue to increase it becomes imperative that we do everything possible to improve the quality and quantity of produce from its gardens. Earthworms and the work they do constitute one of the cheapest and easiest ways of returning goodness to the soil, and apart from a little lime earthworms can work without expensive additions of fertilisers.

> Earthworms are not miracle workers. Although they do soil a power of good, they need help in their work. But if they have help they can slowly improve soil structure, increase moisture retention and help ease erosion, make the soil crumblier so that precious air can reduce sourness, and increase the humus in topsoil to make it more fertile. They can do all of these things, but not without your help.

To repeat, earthworms alter the physical structure of the soil by eating and burrowing their way through it, aerating and granulating it, making it looser and crumblier, and increasing the spaces between the soil particles. This allows better rainwater absorption and greater water stability. Crops will grow better where there is more space for root development, and the altered structure, increased aeration and greater moisture content of the soil encourage better growth and higher yields.

Where large amounts of organic debris are made available as food, earthworms will eat their way through it, increasing the soil fertility by releasing organic nutrients. Where multi-species colonise, a vertical exchange aids the mixing process by bringing up the ingested subsoil minerals and casting the lot in the topsoil layers.

Keeping up soil fertility where cropping is continual may be difficult unless precautionary measures are taken. While in theory it might be possible to fill your cropping fields with earthworm-rich populations, their numbers will reduce sharply unless the organic matter content is continually supplied.

Earthworms can survive in soils where pesticides are applied providing the organic matter is high. Some of the fungicides and herbicides are toxic however. Horticulturalists and orchardists have told me that continual cropping has reduced crop returns severely and resulted in low fertility soils so fine that they can blow away even without a decent wind. Again, the need for applying mulches and organic matter is obvious.

But the dichotomy is that while the soil blows away when it is dry, this kind of run-down soil clods and clumps together when it rains heavily. The soil's ability to 'hang loose' depends very much on its physical properties and fertility. Once organic material is applied — animal manures, compost, mulches or hay, earthworms will help, and soil fertility can be restored and improved.

When possible, applying castings or organic compost including vermicast can be a tremendous aid. You can buy this kind of compost from Trevor Hellyer's Wonderworm Farm in Hawke's Bay at such a low price I am surprised he ever has any to sell.

Where earthworms have helped to rectify soil structure and low soil fertility, especially when castings have been incorporated into the soil, the improvement in plant growth can be little short of amazing. I have no desire to grow monstrous carrots and huge stalks of rhubarb, but I mentioned previously my own experiments with begonias and gloxinias using both earthworms and a variable mix of castings and conventional potting material (see page 61).

More and more New Zealand farmers and growers are turning to organic or biodynamic farming, stating their concerns about the 'environmental, economic and social impacts of chemical or conventional agriculture. Both [organic and biodynamic farming] use no synthetic chemical fertilisers or pesticides, use compost additions and manures to improve soil quality, control pests naturally, rotate crops, and diversify crops and livestock.'

What happens to the earthworm population when organic or biodynamic principles are embraced is quite startling, as the following research shows.

'From 30 soil cores (15 cm in diameter by 15 cm deep) taken on each paddock, we found the biodynamically farmed soil to average 175 earthworms per square metre compared with 21 earthworms per square metre on the conventionally farmed soil. By mass, the biodynamically farmed soil had 86.3 g of earthworms per square metre, whereas the conventionally farmed soil had 3.4 g of earthworms per square metre. These differences were most likely due to *the use of pesticides* [my emphasis], shown to reduce earthworm populations on the conventional farm.'

If you need further convincing of the efficacy of organic and biodynamic enterprises, in most cases they have soils of higher biological and physical quality — higher organic matter content and microbial activity, more earthworms, better soil structure, lower bulk density, easier penetrability and thicker topsoil.

Almost ten years ago PAPA Gardens became the first New Zealand herb farm licensed to apply the internationally recognised 'Demeter' trademark to their products. This trademark is only granted when the products meet the stringent standards of national biodynamic associations.

While biodynamic farmers, following the principles of Rudolf Steiner, use specific preparations made from cow manure, silica and various plants, organic farmers rely on companion planting, organic fertilisers, biological controls and mulching — a natural interchange which encourages harmony with the living soil environment of earthworms and soil microlife.

Mulching is a key component because the continual build-up of organic material on top of the soil encourages the surface feeders and topsoil dwellers to cast in the top 5–10 cm of soil. Mulch conserves the surface moisture, reduces high summer ground temperatures and increases winter temperatures by insulating the soil. The use of mulches promotes a sympathetic temperature range for earthworms and reduces the competition from weeds. Organic gardening is a prime model for crop harvesting where the roots are left behind as worm food, providing vertical distribution of nutrients to lower levels.

While it may take time to convert the ravaged soils of cropland and orchards back to fertility there are a few factors which might speed things along, and your task will be easier if an earthworm farm is considered an integral part of management practice.

The farm should include not only *E. foetida*, the major composting worm, but also *L. rubellus*, the red common or garden worm, and *L. terrestris*, the nightcrawler. Although *L. rubellus* breeds at a slower rate than *E. foetida*, especially in a farmed situation, you

A visit to Paul and Pauline van Eybergen's biodynamic herb farm south of Whangarei is a tranquil experience and a lesson in how herb farming ought to be. Worms, chooks, bees, lush growth, old-world power-packed medicinal and fragrant herbs have become at one with the environment. The van Eybergens are convinced that the organic, biodynamic and permaculture principles they follow ensure the high quality of the herbs from which they make their teas, extracts, tinctures and essential oils.

can bed the two together because they need similar situations. You will need a different environment for *L. terrestris*, and it is worth getting it right because if you can breed this worm and eventually colonise it naturally in orchards, you will have wonderful burrowing activity underground and heaps of castings on top, fabulous fertiliser for your trees.

L. terrestris also buries leaves and fallen fruit and has been shown to reduce some pests and diseases by 'cleaning' the orchard floor.

BREEDING *LUMBRICUS TERRESTRIS*

Although *L. terrestris* makes very deep burrows it is a surface feeder and breeder. A 20- to 30-cm-deep bed is sufficient because this is not to be their lifetime home, and you want them to feed and breed on the surface, not encourage them to burrow and tunnel. If you use standard bedding, add plenty of extra dried cow or horse manure, or make up special bedding of two parts aged crushed cow or horse manure, two parts sawdust, untreated, and one part dried and crushed leaves. Replace the sawdust with chopped and decomposing lawn clippings if you like. Add 220 g/m^2 of lime and mix thoroughly, wetting and mixing until it is fluffy and damp, not soggy. Let it age or heat.

Place the bedding in the bin, level the top, and introduce the earthworms, which are difficult to collect at night unless you use a filtered red light. Turn the bed once a week by forking and turning it upside down. Always level it. Sprinkle water daily to keep the bedding surface damp so the worms will come up to feed.

Topfeed with fresh manure, crushed or ground leaves and lawn clippings. (Grated carrot, chocolate? Treat!) They will enjoy small amounts of fresh short green lawn clippings. Add food little and often, only as much as will be cleaned up in 24 hours. Grain feed should not be necessary and do not feed with sewer sludge.

When harvesting to put the worms under the trees, make sure the area you are transferring them to duplicates the bed conditions as far as possible, until they have adjusted to the soil. Take all the large worms out of the bed, rake the bedding flat again, water and continue feeding as before. Do not harvest again for four or five weeks, then repeat the procedure.

Because *L. terrestris* likes to wander, hence the nightcrawler nickname, keep the soil around the bed as dry as possible. If you notice your charges out of bed, keep a light on to discourage them.

When transferring *any* farmed worms into crop soil or under trees it is essential to keep supplying the organic food as a mulch cover, keep up the moisture level and maintain the pH with lime. Sprinkling the transplant area with a liquid fish or blood and bone fertiliser after the daily water sprinkling will help them establish themselves.

GREEN MANURES

Green manures like clovers, mustards and ryes are another tool you can use to rid soil of the effects of pesticides and improve soil structure and fertility. Earthworms love them.

Good soil is at the heart of organic growing and green manures can make a real difference to the soil and the plants grown in it. While they are sometimes regarded as space wasters, that view is short-sighted when you consider the benefits a green crop can return to soil, especially where manure supplies, compost and bulky organic debris may be hard to get.

Light sandy soils probably benefit the most from green manures as humus build-up is gained and soil structure improved by digging the crop into the ground and adding as much nitrogenous manure as possible. Left to decompose, nitrogen and other nutrients so essential to plant growth are released. Instead of letting land lie fallow, say in early autumn, plant a green manure crop after harvesting. The soil will still be warm and earthworms and the microlife will still be active, cleaning up any plant residue.

Green manure crops should be left to grow for as long as possible, being dug in just before they start to turn woody. Leaving them longer than this will make them harder to turn in and they will take longer to decompose. Should this happen cut the top off and leave it to mulch, or put it through the compost heap. Of course you can chop the crop about, leaving the roots below ground, and leave the earthworms to pull the mulching, decomposing material into the soil.

Farmers can sow a green crop like mustard or alfalfa under corn, once the corn is a few inches high. When the corn crop is harvested in the early autumn, the green crop will be well established and ready to give good insulation during winter. The corn stubble should be ground and used as winter cover and food for worms.

SHEET COMPOSTING

Another tool to improve and rebuild impoverished soil before crops are planted is sheet composting, which is made in the ground instead of in the heap.

All of the materials you would normally use in building a compost heap are laid on the ground and either dug in or run over and chopped up by a rotovator and buried to a depth of 10 cm. Within three months the material will have rotted sufficiently for planting to take place.

I have never done this, and while I can see the practicality of this method the number of top-dwelling earthworms that could be decimated in the rotovating process concerns me. I daresay that in low fertility soils there would be few earthworms and after all that is what sheet composting is all about, to improve impoverished soil. I don't believe I would use this method where there were plenty of earthworms. I would instead spread the materials on top of the ground, cover them with hay, leave them to decompose and then plant in three months' time, much like no-dig gardening.

However, the sheet composting method does have the advantage of rebuilding garden soil quickly and in the ground, so there is little nutrient loss. I suppose this is just an expanded method of digging a corner of the garden, tossing in a bucket of kitchen waste and replacing the soil.

MAKING THE MOST OF EARTHWORMS IN ORCHARDS

You will have to look elsewhere for ways to treat codlin moth, leaf rollers or lichen, but a more balanced soil may help trees produce a higher resistance to plant diseases and pests. Fruit trees which have never borne fruit may well become productive after earthworms have established colonies around and under the trees, and helped remedy deficiencies in the soil.

Earthworms like to work in the shade, among the fine roots of trees, taking nourishment from the leaf drop and the vast bacterial life in the soil. This is one of the reasons why shelter belts and old tree plantations are possible source material when looking for beneficial worms to transplant.

Because earthworms have this liking for trees and shade there is a natural advantage when using earthworms in orchards. Another advantage occurs because the tree roots, especially of citrus, do not respond favourably to cultivating. By cooperating with both the trees' and the earthworms' natural preferences and simply adding sufficient moisture, animal manures, organic fertilisers, organic

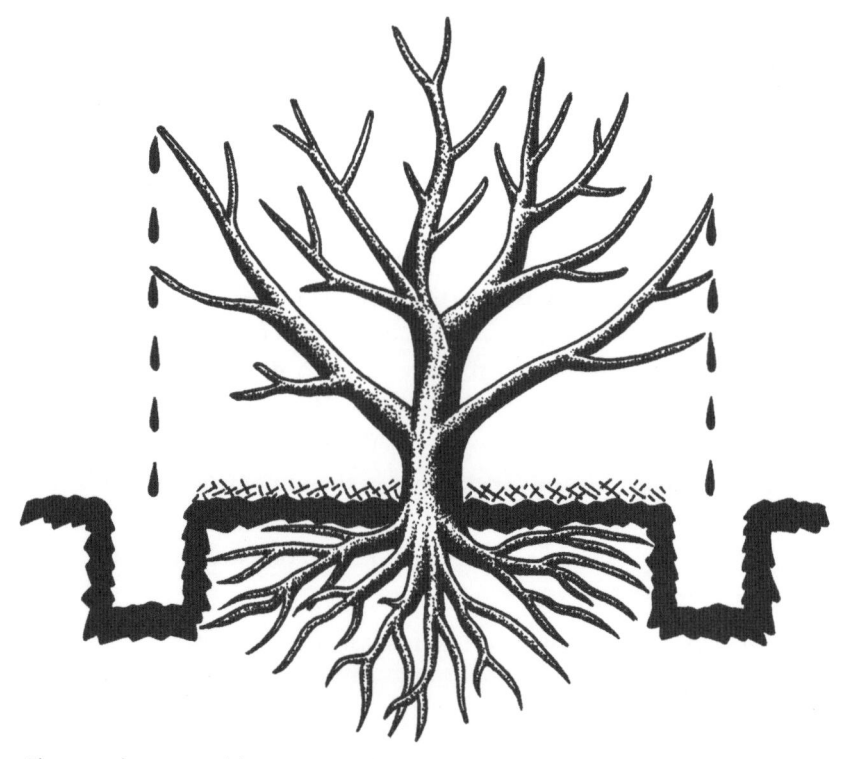

Plant earthworms with extra organic
material at the drip line of orchard trees.

mulch and lime or dolomite for the pH, you can almost watch the trees grow. (And there should be little need for pesticides.) This will increase the productivity, the soil depth and the numbers of earthworms.

Here are three simple guidelines to a mutually beneficial life for earthworms and fruiting trees.

1. Stop cultivating around trees.

2. As most fruit tree roots extend to the circumference of the tree, rake any leaves from under trees and mound them around the perimeter beneath the outer drip line where the soil remains damper longer.

3. Use a push hoe to keep the weeds down and never let them go to seed. As the worm population increases leave them where they have been chopped. Until then, rake them to the perimeter or cover them with a mulch.

The earthworm population will rapidly increase and you will have one huge, slightly puggy earthworm bed. In the meantime you can help it along by transplanting *L. terrestris* and *L. rubellus* from the worm beds. Eventually you will be able to use *L. terrestris* to fish with while the trees grow.

Everything about this mutual cooperation in the orchard is pleasing, from lower fertiliser and labour costs, a shorter period of time to fruiting, greater yields of quality fruit, a longer life for the orchard and a genuine regard for and contribution to the environment.

Earthworm farming

Whenever I have attempted to save or breed native earthworms brought to me by 'kind' people removing them from their natural environment they have eventually gone into a steady decline and died. It has been impossible, for me at least, to reproduce a compatible environment for them to breed in.

There's a lesson there, in that of our approximately 185 native species not one is dominant over any of the introduced European species, except where their environment is alien to the Lumbricidae. And even in their own surroundings, it can still take decades for a native species to spread from a single breeding colony and fully permeate an acre of ground.

Many of the native, leaf mould, non-burrowing species lived in indigenous forests and it became difficult for them to thrive once New Zealand became a grassland economy. But this same grassland economy, similar to the green green grass of home, with a lack of ground predators and a mainly temperate climate, made it easy for the European species, arriving as egg capsules in the roots of trees and in the soil ballast of early ships, to adapt and establish themselves in New Zealand.

Early population counts show that imported species were quickly able to establish themselves in pasture in populations of around ten worms per cubic foot — one million worms per acre — and in ideal situations the populations could be three million worms per acre or higher.

In my small and experimental earthworm farm, using commercially bred *E. foetida* (tigers) and *L. rubellus* (reds), I had an average population density of 1,000–1,500 per cubic foot. More efficient farmers can reach levels of 3,000 worms per cubic foot.

BREEDING THE RIGHT STOCK

Be sure you are breeding the correct stock for the purpose. People still get confused about the differences between composters and earthworkers, and about the suitability of commercially produced composters to improve pasture soils.

If you want earthworms to reduce huge quantities of organic waste to vermicompost or castings, in landfills, food producing and processing plants, household waste, abattoirs, pig, dairy and stable wastes or sewage treatment plants; to reduce the possibility of fungal diseases in orchard waste; for zoos, aquariums and pet shops, poultry and bird breeders or fisheries; for compost heaps and composting toilets, you will need to breed *composting worms*, that is, *E. foetida*, *E. rosea*, and to a lesser extent *L. rubellus*.

If you want earthworms to build soil and fertility, improve gardens, pasture, forestlands, orchards, croplands and crop yields, land values, for castings or for fishing bait, you need *earthworkers*. That is, *A. caliginosa, longa, trapezoides, rosea, chlorotica, O. cyaneum, L. terrestris* and *rubellus*. Limited breeding of *A. caliginosa* and *longa* is possible. *L. terrestris* is difficult but worthwhile persevering with, and *L. rubellus* is easy to breed. I do not know of anyone breeding *A. chlorotica* or *O. cyaneum*.

You may add or transplant composters to gardens, pasture and croplands, but unless high quantities of rich organic material are

---

If you consider that one active breeding worm with its progeny is capable of producing 1,000–1,500 earthworms within a 12-month period, you can see that a rapid pyramiding of density is possible within a short space of time. If the food and accommodation offered is adequate and hospitable, and the temperature and moisture conditions are suitable, quality breeding stock will proliferate and work the year through.

available or can be incorporated into the soil when the worms are introduced, *E. foetida* will not survive for long and its major value will be in the protein added to the soil by the dead bodies. *L. rubellus* should survive if the conditions are suitable because it is both a composter and a surface dweller.

Propagating earthworms

I always advise prospective earthworm farmers to start with a small number of breeders so that they can get to know the small creatures' preferences without killing them off. Just as it is difficult to learn to ride a bicycle from a book, a manual about earthworm breeding can only give you the basics. You need to start small so that you can put the suggestions and principles into practice, find your way through the traps and learn as much as possible about your stock before expanding. No doubt there are many things I do which other earthworm breeders would frown upon, and the reverse is certainly true. In any case you may find that you hate handling earthworms.

Knowledge brings confidence, and only once you have that should you buy plenty of breeders or egg capsules. The labour necessary to handle large numbers of worms isn't much greater than for small numbers. If you are planning to go into earthworm farming in a big way, the more breeders you start with the faster you can get into intensive production.

When breeding intensively you can harvest plenty of castings and egg capsules either to sell or to add directly to the soil. Your venture can establish a sympathetic relationship between the soil-dwelling beneficial earthworkers and the farmed composting earthworms. By using the composters' output you can encourage

> Earthworkers or soil dwellers are not as easy to breed as composters because the conditions under which they will proliferate are not as easy to reproduce. But incorporating the castings produced by the composters into pastures and gardens will certainly increase the soil porosity and fertility and will make the soil more hospitable for earthworkers to populate.

the earthworkers' soil-building activities. Put simply, earthworkers like fertile soil and castings help make it more friable and the nutrients more accessible to plant growth. Assuming that you are providing your composters with enough of the right organic material you should confidently expect to get populations of around 3,000 worms per cubic foot.

A word of caution, however. No doubt you will have a business plan but be sure you know exactly where you are heading, and where you are going to sell your stock, egg capsules, castings or whatever. Don't breed up large populations and then look around for a market. Do your homework first and initiate new prospects and projects.

To continually achieve high, healthy populations in such limited space, the food and bedding supplied for them to live in and work through needs to be of a high quality. Giving them bedding consisting mainly of shredded paper will provide warmth and air but little in the way of nourishment. Adding horse manure, lawn clippings and a bit of compost will improve the accommodation rating markedly. Feeding your stock on a diet composed solely of lawn clippings probably ensures their survival if they don't get bored, but may not see them thrive and breed enthusiastically.

Similarly, if you plan to transplant very young worms directly into the soil, and want them to live and thrive, the soil must be rich in organic material similar to that in which they have been bred. If these guidelines are followed the surviving composters and resident earthworkers will improve and build soil faster than nature, although they will need your help in supplying masses of organic material and keeping the pH sensitive.

Think about the way cows, horses, pigs and sheep — the stock on top of the ground — respond to high grade treatment. The stock in your beds and bins is no different. Withholding the right stuff to make them thrive is shortsighted and most unkind to the worms.

EGG CAPSULE PRODUCTION
Many new colonies of earthworms have been started when

capsules swallowed by birds have been dropped on high mountaintops or on islands throughout the seven seas; transported from one place to another stuck to soil on the hoofs or hides of animals; accidentally taken thousands of miles from their place of origin on the roots of plants and trees; or scattered by the wind to new locations and out-of-the-way places. That is almost certainly how the imported lumbricids arrived in New Zealand, among the roots of deciduous trees being carried to the colonies by the more affluent settlers.

Under the right temperature and moisture conditions, the normal incubation period for egg capsules is about two to three weeks, but with deliberate sun or air drying they may remain dormant but fertile for eighteen months or more. Applying moisture and warmth will encourage them to swell and develop.

Capsules may also be refrigerated at low temperatures until they are required. In cold and freezing climates, huge numbers of dormant capsules will hatch from manure piles, compost heaps and the earth as soon as spring arrives and the soil heats up. Similarly, where drought conditions have prevailed, dormant capsules are stimulated into hatching after drought-breaking rains. The ability of fertile egg capsules to lie dormant is one of the reasons for the heavy distribution of earthworms over the earth. It also makes it possible to produce earthworm egg-capsules commercially and ship them anywhere in the world.

If you remove mature earthworms to a new environment they will probably die, unless it is similar to the old. Compost- and manure-bred worms need compost and manure; soil-bred worms need soil enriched with vegetable and mineral matter. This is a fact whether we are talking about native, imported or farm-bred

Deciding to set up a sideline of concentrated egg capsule production may be ideal for a city farmer, especially in areas where landscape gardeners do lots of work. This seems to me a potentially captive market, and would no doubt improve the survival rate of many new and transplanted trees.

earthworms. However, in the case of farm-bred worms, if you remove them when they are small, before they have become used to continual supplies of food, you will have a better chance of them surviving, adapting and eventually breeding and colonising new areas.

Even better, use their adaptability in the earlier stage, and engage in intensive egg-capsule production. When placed in a new environment, the capsules will hatch tiny worms well able to adapt to the soil in which they are born.

EARTHWORM FARMING

The small city gardener may have only a few square feet of garden, or possibly just a few potted plants or a windowbox to work with. Others may have a vegetable or flower garden, a market garden or nursery, and so on up to gardeners with extensive areas of orchard or farm.

Earthworm farming may be engaged in successfully on any scale, whether it be for producing fine potting material for a few plants, a small garden or for a big acreage. A start may be made in a small box with a few earthworm eggs or worms. The technique really is the same, regardless of the size or the surroundings. All that alters is the volume of bedding and food required to service the project.

Bedding material

I've previously written extensively about bedding so I'll just recap here. The bedding I most favour for a high breeding environment usually consists of about equal quantities of rotting hay, cold horse, cow or sheep manure, lawn clippings and almost-ready compost, tired soil or recycled castings. I add lime, a packet of wheatgerm and a packet of cornmeal or a couple of handfuls of grain left over from making bread — oat bran, wholemeal, kibbled wheat, bulghur wheat — and mix the whole thoroughly with sufficient water to make it fluffy and moist. Bedding recipes are many and various. This is what I like to use.

If I want to be able to remove the egg capsules more easily or speed up the production of castings I use less fibrous material and more manure, and for egg capsule boxes I include pre-soaked peat moss, extra cornmeal which seems to help produce firm, large capsules, and small quantities of grated lard which the worms rapidly clean up. Adding fats is frowned upon by some growers but if it is hard and fresh I will use it in small quantities.

Feeding and watering
There is plenty of sustenance in the bedding to provide nourishment while the worms are settling in, but after a week or so I topfeed once a week, usually with horse manure or whatever is freely available. If you do not use a separate earthworm bin for disposing of kitchen waste, it is excellent food and may be spread evenly on the surface, sprinkled with lime and covered with a thin layer of soil. Do not add meat products which can encourage flies. Keep up the water sprinkling, although kitchen and greengrocer waste contains a lot of moisture and you do not want the bed soggy. But earthworms cannot eat dry food and if you let the bed dry out the whole system will slow down, lessening breeding and therefore egg capsule production. Keeping the bed covered with old moist carpet, blankets, sweaters or sacking will conserve moisture and provide some insulation and darkness. The worms will eventually eat the covering.

USING EARTHWORMS IN THE WASTE INDUSTRY
While the withdrawn earthworkers do their best for the environment by taking care of and improving the soil, the jostling composters wait in the wings to be pressed into service to do what they do best, dispose of waste. By and large, however, they wait in vain.

If you want to know how New Zealand industries and local authorities have utilised earthworms to convert organic waste matter to vermicast the answer is simple. They have barely scratched the surface. In fact it's worse than that. With the exception of the Christchurch City Council and the Wellington City Council, who are at least triers, most of the organisations responsible for waste management haven't even begun to contemplate, let alone examine seriously, the uses of composting earthworms in waste management.

— *Earthworm farming* —

Serious earthworm farmers must themselves encourage the use of worms in these and other industries, and initiate potential markets. We've got stuck on castings for potting mix and in gardens, and earthworms for fish and bird food. We haven't begun to look at other possibilities such as developing dried earthworm protein for cattle meal, or fresh earthworm protein for food in Third World countries. Lateral thinkers are few and far between.

To return to the realm of the possible, with the exception of companies who use non-organic materials like plastics or metals, virtually every other industry in this country, and certainly every food processing industry or plant, should be looking at harnessing earthworms to rid themselves of an expensive and land-hogging necessity — rubbish.

Perhaps it isn't their fault and there simply has not been sufficient information to encourage people into trials. Perhaps if they knew about composting earthworms they would at least install

---

In other countries fishing bait is one of the major products of many earthworm farms. I'm not sure why but it hasn't quite caught on here, except for the coarse fishing clubs who are delighted to use worms for bait. Whatever the reason for the non-flourishing wormbait industry, it is becoming clear that within ten years fish farming or aquaculture should be a booming industry and a potent export earner. With the move to formalise the wild eel fishing industry in New Zealand, one component of this expected growth will be in the freshwater culturing of eels and eel farms, and earthworms, especially *L. rubellus*, *L. terrestris* and *E. foetida*, as the superior natural food source should make this style of farming more commercially viable.

Although a lateral progression, converting worm protein into 'upmarket' eel flesh is a distinct possibility, especially where the worms are already part of the eels' natural food. Eels thrive on them.

As the planet becomes more and more polluted, the cultural food needs of Maori and other nations will make the farming of eel and other freshwater species commercially viable, and no doubt the humble earthworm will play its part in this development.

a small pilot scheme to examine the possibility. And perhaps they wouldn't. Maybe the problem continues to be filed in the 'too hard' basket.

But as costs continue to rise in most areas, innovative Kiwis will need to continue to find new ways to do things, and perhaps they could be persuaded to put farmed composting earthworms at the top of the list. Use the freeze dry process to extract moisture from worm bodies, follow up the tantalising research work of extracting a fine oil suitable in the treatment of heart disease (or am I just gullible?), develop pleasing waterless waste-reducing toilets using earthworms, or simply put the earthworms to work to improve that clean green image that we like to boast about. Rubbish and waste disposal is just a start. Don't be bound by your imagination.

New Zealand worm farmers

There are now many people interested in earthworms and earthworm farming who even five years ago would not have treated the idea of breeding earthworms seriously. Even now some people still fall about! Earthworm farming is a business that I believe has a great future but it needs particular sorts of individuals to make it work successfully. Earthworm farming is not for 'get in and get out' merchants who just want to make a quick buck. And it's definitely not for people who do not care about the non-verbal creatures of the earth without whom humankind would not survive.

Since I wrote my first book about earthworm farming I've met or communicated with some thousands of people. Most of them are pleasant, caring individuals who like to garden and who believe that earthworms have something to offer the soil. They know that earthworms are good for the garden, even if they don't know why, and they want to know a little more about breeding them.

There are the starry-eyed of course, those who want to hitch their fortunes to a worm but who don't really think of them as more than a means to an end. There are a couple who went in big and came a cropper. They didn't really care about earthworms either, only money. And there are a number, like Marvyn Smith in Auckland and Sue Wright in Hamilton, who are still working away at their small businesses and gaining satisfaction at what they have chosen to do.

For the most part the successful earthworm farmers are a little quirky, people who like the unexpected and a bit of a challenge, and people who are committed to earthworms, not for money, power or prestige, but because they believe that earthworms have a lot to offer. I hope they will not mind my saying that they are quirky. There are not very many of them so far. There will be more, but it is worth mentioning three whom I know reasonably well.

Perhaps John Stemmer of Rangimarie Worm Farm in Motueka will not want to be known as the father of earthworm farming in New Zealand, but from where I sit, John is it. I don't want letters from people telling me that their grandfather bred earthworms 70 years ago. I've no doubt that other people bred earthworms long before John Stemmer came on the scene, but what John has done has been to make many people aware of the power of this fragile creature. Think about it. Can you seriously believe that a scrap of wriggling protein has more power to convert rubbish into goodness than you have?

John Stemmer has been making people aware of that power for nigh on twenty years. I don't know if he even knows how many earthworms or tonnes of castings he has sold, how many people he has made look at the earthworm in a different light, how many gardens his earthworms and castings have improved, how many people, like me, have bought 2,000 earthworms from John to make a start. In my own case those 2,000 earthworms set me on a voyage of discovery.

When he started all those years ago John had an idea and a dream. He was a real pioneer in this business, and he probably knows more about earthworms than anybody else in New Zealand. His knowledge isn't confined to the composting species he mainly breeds. John has a fund of knowledge about *A. caliginosa* which he plans to reveal in a future book about pasture worms. I really hope he writes this book so that we can all learn more.

John has gained his knowledge through trial and error over a long period of time, much of it with little income, and he would be the first person to say that he is still learning. That's another thing about great worm farmers. They are always ready to learn something new. When you think about it isn't that what all professionals have in common, whether their field is law, science, building, or worm farming?

John's farm in the Brooklyn Valley is not huge but it contains sufficient beds to turn over millions of earthworms and their castings every year. I visited Rangimarie Worm Farm the day after Motueka had had about 100 mm of rain and the area was a shocking sight. Even so, the worms were about their business and life was proceeding, as it does in the world of earthworms.

The weather was quite different when I visited Trevor Hellyer at Wonder Worm Farm in Hastings. It was a sticky late summer Hawke's Bay day and much of the region was dry and parched. At the worm farm all was pretty green and my first sight of Trevor was as he manoeuvred a huge tractor around monstrous piles of organic compost.

If John Stemmer's farm is compact, by comparison Trevor Hellyer's is huge. Trevor has now been earthworm farming for twelve years, and he has mechanised his production as much as is possible.

There are four major components to the business: organic compost composed of broken down worm castings and organic material; worms and castings which he sells together in a 10-litre or so mix; straight castings, sterilised and power packed, and a compost mix of peat, soil and castings.

To me, perhaps the most interesting part of his operation is his acre and a half of windrowed composting material. Trevor is fortunate to have dumped at his place a waste product from the freezing works, the paunch grass from the first stomach of slaughtered cattle. I had never seen or heard of anything like it. Spread in long mounded rows it takes twelve months to convert to a wonderful organic compost through which first *E. foetida* has grazed and feasted on, followed by *L. rubellus*.

Trevor mentioned something in passing which a couple of researchers have written about — a substance which *E. foetida* seems to exude which prepares the compost for *L. rubellus*, in its surface grazing and soil mixing capacity, to start working. At some stage down the line *A. caliginosa* enters and has a turn.

It's a wonderful cooperative effort on the part of the earthworms and the organic compost is just the best stuff, which Trevor sells for the incredibly low price of $25 for 600 litres. And I didn't have a trailer! I'm amazed that he ever has any to sell but the locals seem to take Trevor and his worms for granted, not appreciating what they have on their doorsteps.

Trevor's earthworm bedding and food is the almost decomposed material mixed with a good lashing off another huge pile of waste — the trimmings, fats and remains of other works' waste that is not allowed into the sewage system. I didn't want to enquire too closely. In the beds the earthworms writhed. I have never seen so many.

Trevor is one of those guys who will tackle anything. Need a machine? He'll make it. He made his own vibrating and rotating casting and worm sorting machine having seen one in a visit to a farm in the US. Got a problem? Ask Trevor. He'll have a good idea of how to solve it. There are quite a number of men in New Zealand with those special talents and it's great that earthworm farming has attracted Trevor Hellyer.

Robin Whitta of Robin's Worms in Howick, Auckland, is a newcomer to the business but what strides he has made since he was attracted to earthworm farming in October 1994.

An ex-builder who was looking for a new challenge, Robin Whitta has built his farm in the basement of his house in Howick. It is a most cleverly designed arrangement of, at this time, about twelve baths, stacking bins and a rapid breeder which he built from a picture in David Murphy's book *Earthworms in Australia.*

Each bath in full production is capable of carrying about 20,000 worms, but his rapid breeder makes the replacement of stock a continuous cycle.

The worms are fed on dried, almost composted pig manure and appear to like the experience. Robin wants to concentrate on selling castings and liquid worm manure, an ideal compromise to make in a city situation. I am trying to tell him that egg capsules are the way to go but I haven't convinced him yet.

Robin's really special skill is in his ability to learn quickly and put what he learns into practice. He is getting a real charge out of what he is doing and learning, and he has a remarkable ability to get other farmers and interested parties together.

As a city breeder Robin has a few problems to overcome but he also has the advantage of being very close to a huge market. If people can find out where he is he should do really well.

In the huge education process needed to get earthworm farming and utilisation really off the ground in this country, these guys can help.

Bibliography

Barrett, Thomas J., *Harnessing the Earthworm*. Bookworm Publishing, P.O. Box 655, Ontario, California 91761.

Buckerfield, John C., *Management of Appropriate Earthworms for Agriculture & Vermiculture*. CSIRO, Division of Soils, Urrbrae, South Australia. Technical Report No. 2/1994.

Campbell, Stu, *Let It Rot: The Home Gardener's Guide to Composting*. Garden Way Publishing, Charlotte, Vermont 05445, 1975.

Dale, Patrick, *A Houseful of Strangers: Living with the Common Creatures of the NZ House & Garden*. Harper Collins, Auckland, 1992.

Hopp, Henry, *What Every Gardener Should Know About Earthworms*. Garden Way Associates Inc., 1978.

Lee, K.E., *The Earthworm Fauna of New Zealand*. NZ Dept of Scientific & Industrial Research, Bulletin 130. Government Printer, 1959.

Morgan, Charlie, *Profitable Earthworm Farming: Complete Manual of Worm Production, Storage, Selling and Shipping*. Shields Publications, PO Box 669, Eagle River, Wisconsin 54521. Gen. Ed. John Bond.

Mother Earth Manual of Organic Gardening. Reed, 1976.

Ridley, Mark (Ed.), 'The Formation of Vegetable Mould Through the Action of Worms'. In *The Essential Darwin*. Unwin Hyman Ltd, 1987.

Shields, Earl B., *Raising Earthworms for Profit*. Shields Publications,

P.O. Box 669, Eagle River, Wisconsin 54521.

Windust, Allan, *Worms Downunder Downunder: For Farm, Garden, Schools, Profit & Recycling*. Allscape, Mandurang, Victoria 3551, Australia, 1994.

NEW ZEALAND RESEARCH PAPERS

Hamblyn, C.J., Dingwall, A.R., 'Earthworms.' *NZ Journal of Agriculture* 71:53, 1945.

Martin, N.A., Charles, J.C., 'Lumbricid Earthworms and Cattle Dung in NZ Pastures.' Proc. of the 2nd Australasian Conference on Grassland Invertebrate Ecology, 1979.

Reganold, J.P., Palmer, A.S., Lockhart, J.C., Macgregor, A.N., 'Soil Quality and Financial Performance of Biodynamic and Conventional Farms In NZ.' *Science* 260, 1993.

Stockdill, S.M.J., 'The Effect of Earthworms on Pastures.' *Proceedings of the NZ Ecological Society* 13: 68-75, 1966.

Stockdill, S.M.J., 'Soils Earthworm Introduction.' Aglink FPP 211, 1984.

Springett, J.A., 'A New Method for Extracting Earthworms from Soilcores, with a Comparison of Four Commonly Used Methods for Estimating Earthworm Populations.' Pedobiologia 21, 217-222. 1981..

Springett, J.A., 'Potential Value of Exotic Earthworms In NZ Soils.' Report of Meeting at Invermay Research Station 27-28 October 1982.

Waters, R.A.S., 'Earthworms and the Fertility of Pasture.' *NZ Grasslands Association* 13: 168-175, 1951.

Wilson, Boyd, 'Time, Lime and Earthworms.' *NZ Farmer*, November 1984.